West Chicago Public Library District
118 West Washington
West Chicago, IL 60185-2803
Phone # (630) 231-1552

THE TWITTER HISTORY OF THE WORLD

First published in 2009

This edition published in 2015 by Prion
an imprint of the Carlton Publishing Group
20 Mortimer Street
London W1T 3JW

Text copyright © 2009 Mitch Benn & Jon Holmes
Design and layout © 2009, 2015 Carlton Books Limited

A CIP catalogue record for this book is available from the British Library.
The publishers would like to thank the following sources for their kind permission to reproduce the pictures in this book:
Key: t=Top, b=Bottom, c=Centre, l=Left and r=Right
Getty Images: /AFP: 124, /The Bridgeman Art Library: 44, /Tim Graham: 127, /Hulton Archive: 52, 74, /Keystone: 114, /Michael Ochs Archives: 123, /Popperfoto: 108, 111, /Time & Life Pictures: 94, 120.
istockphoto.com: 72, 73, 81, /Gary Blakeley: 110, /George Clerk: 50, /Rene Drouyer: 90, /Volkan Ersoy: 109, /Hedda Gjerpen: 8, /Mihail Glushkov: 98, /Christina Hanck: 66, /Arie J. Jager: 106, /Stefan Klein: 128, /Liz Leyden: 96, /Peter Lora: 91, /Ray Roper: 88, /Dario Rota: 61, /Vincent Voight: 67, /Duncan Walker: 48, 78, /Steven Wynn: 76, 86.

Every effort has been made to acknowledge correctly and contact the source and/or copyright holder of each picture and Carlton Books Limited apologises for any unintentional errors or omissions which will be corrected in future editions of this book.

ISBN: 978 1 85375 932 1

Printed in Dubai

THE TWITTER HISTORY OF THE WORLD

Tweets from God, John Lennon and many more...

MITCH BENN & JON HOLMES

PRION

CONTENTS

IN-TWEET-DUCTION BY
MITCH BENN & JON HOLMES

Over Easter 2009, largely to amuse himself, Jon spent a silly amount of time tweeting from the perspective of Jesus, as if Jesus had woken up in the tomb with only his Blackberry for company. What would Christ tweet to his followers (he had 12) while he was waiting for the stone to be rolled away, and should he or shouldn't he draw a self portrait on his shroud in permanent marker pen?

Upon reading this, Mitch came up with the staggeringly simple notion of 'tweeting through history' and writing it all in a book. He had the idea on the A12 in the middle of the night and phoned Jon from a service station to tell him. Next day they met in Starbucks and formulated a plan. The rest, just like the subject of the book, is history.

@mitchbenn
@jonholmes1

August 2009

FORE-TWEET BY
STEPHEN FRY

stephenfry An achievement of almost imponderable
complexity, ambiguity, depth, emotional charge and delicately
nuanced sensitivity, this certainly isn'
8:32 AM 16th Jul 2009 from FryPhone

#THECREATION
OFTHEUNIVERSE

GOD Let there be light!
9:00 AM 1st Jan 14,452,319 BC from Godberry

GOD Morning all... @creation
9:01 AM 1st Jan 14,452,319 BC from Godberry

GOD ... and let there be lunch.
12:06 PM 1st Jan 14,452,319 BC from Godberry

GOD Better crack on with this, I suppose.
1:31 PM 1st Jan 14,452,319 BC from Godberry

GOD It says "connect astral plane to physical plane at
interstice b" where's the bloody astral plane? Sodding flatpacks
2:06 PM 1st Jan 14,452,319 BC from Godberry

GOD got it. It had rolled under the sofa (dur face)
2:06 PM 1st Jan 14,452,319 BC from Godberry

GOD Toyed with pink & orange for this little planet,
but bit harsh on the eyes. Blue and green much nicer.
11:24 AM 2nd Jan 14,452,319 BC from Godberry

GOD urgh, fairly sure THAT wasn't meant to happen.
10:03 AM 3rd Jan 14,452,319 BC from Godberry

GOD D'oh, checked diagrams again and it's BIRDS
of the air and BEASTS of the fields. Bugger, what a mess.
10:12 AM 3rd Jan 14,452,319 BC from Godberry

GOD For a minute there I thought birds would be okay
but beasts landed on them before they could fly off.
Never finish by Saturday at this rate.
10:15 AM 3rd Jan 14,452,319 BC from Godberry

GOD How am I going to get rid of several billion flat animals?
10:19 AM 3rd Jan 14,452,319 BC from Godberry

GOD Hold on, got an idea.
10:23 AM 3rd Jan 14,452,319 BC from Godberry

GOD Just on a hunch tried "let there be fewer flat animals".
Worked like a charm. Off to make some more.
11:02 AM 3rd Jan 14,452,319 BC from Godberry

GOD Knackered. Putting feet up 2moro, tweet day after.
5:04 PM 5th Jan 14,452,319 BC from Godberry

GOD I suppose you're wondering
what this is all about? And quite right too.
9:30 PM 7th Jan 14,452,319 BC from Godberry

GOD Wondering is the whole idea. If I just told you
everything now, that would be no fun at all,
would it? Certainly not for me.
9:32 PM 7th Jan 14,452,319 BC from Godberry

GOD Oh, and don't worry about that BC
business in the date. Just something I'm working on for later.
9:33 AM 7th Jan 14,452,319 BC from Godberry

GOD @creation In the meantime, have a look round, enjoy
yourselves, keep evolving and await further instructions.
Bye now! God out x
9:36 AM 7th Jan 14,452,319 BC from Godberry

#MONOCELLULAR LIFEFORMS

Glob22456 @Glob87587 Have you seen @Glob56128 recently?
12:13 PM 9th Mar 3,898,675,237 BC from MonoCellPhone

Glob87587 @Glob22456 Yes. What's that thing he keeps waving about at everybody?
12:14 PM 9th Mar 3,898,675,237 BC from ProkaryoteWeb

Glob22456 @Glob87587 It's called a FLAGELLUM, apparently.
12:15 PM 9th Mar 3,898,675,237 BC from MonoCellPhone

Glob87587 @Glob22456 Where'd he get it?
12:16 PM 9th Mar 3,898,675,237 BC from ProkaryoteWeb

Glob22456 @Glob87587 Says he evolved it.
12:17 PM 9th Mar 3,898,675,237 BC from MonoCellPhone

Glob87587 @Glob22456 Wanker.
12:18 PM 9th Mar 3,898,675,237 BC from ProkaryoteWeb

Glob22456 @Glob87587 Yeah. Wanker.
12:19 PM 9th Mar 3,898,675,237 BC from MonoCellPhone

Glob56128 Weeeeeeeeeeeeeeeeeeeeeee.
12.19 PM 9th Mar 3,898,675,237 BC from PrimordialSuperHighway

#THEEXTINCTION OFTHEDINOSAURS

BigT @Trike See the fireworks last night?
10:12 AM 4th Feb 65,276,451BC from TweetRex

Trike @BigT Yeah, pretty good wasn't it? :)
10:13 AM 4th Feb 65,276,451BC from CretaceousWeb

BigT @Trike Weather's a bit rubbish today.
10.14 AM 4th Feb 65,276,451 BC from TweetRex

Trike @BigT Hm. Kinda dark. :(
10:15 AM 4th Feb 65,276,451BC from CretaceousWeb

#ADAMANDEVE

adam just come to life in a garden.
9:00 AM 5th Day from paradiseonline

adam am naked.
9:01 AM 5th Day from paradiseonline

adam must have been some night!
9:02 AM 5th Day from paradiseonline

eve @adam hi adam, I'm following you on twitter.
9:02 AM 5th Day from paradiseonline

adam @eve how did you find me?
9:03 AM 5th Day from paradiseonline

eve @adam because there are only two of us on here.
9:03 AM 5th Day from paradiseonline

adam @eve did, erm, anything happen last night?
9:05 AM 5th Day from paradiseonline

eve @adam you don't remember? Gone all shy??
9:06 AM 5th Day from paradiseonline

adam @eve To be honest, it's all a bit hazy.
Was there a giant snake?
9:07 AM 5th Day from paradiseonline

eve @adam well it wasn't bad big boy but I wouldn't go
so far as to say that ;-)
9:07 AM 5th Day from paradiseonline

adam @eve no, in the tree!
9:08 AM 5th Day from paradiseonline

eve @adam LOL.
9:09 AM 5th Day from paradiseonline

adam @eve There was an apple. I remember you had an apple and
after that everything just kind of seemed to go wrong.
9:10 AM 5th Day from paradiseonline

eve @adam Jesus, typical man. Always blaming the woman.
9:11 AM 5th Day from paradiseonline

adam @eve Alright! chillax. I was only saying. And who's Jesus?
9:12 AM 5th Day rom paradiseonline

eve @adam Well don't. And for your information your serpent is
tiny. I've had bigger tree roots.
9:13 AM 5th Day from paradiseonline

adam @eve what the hell's wrong with you all of a sudden? Time of
the month is it?
9:14 AM 5th Day from paradiseonline

eve @adam Oh piss off.
9:14 AM 5th Day from paradiseonline

#NEANDERTHALS

OG Today Og VERY EXCITED cos today VERY IMPORTANT day. Og new neighbours come for dinner. Og wearing best bumflap (rabbit!)
4:28 PM 12th Feb 65,982 BC from NetAnderthal

Cro-M01 Oh lawks, just remembered—tonight we've agreed to dine with our new "neighbours". Heaven knows what horrors await; one does what one must.
4:31 PM 12th Feb 65,982 BC from SapiensWeb

OG Wonder whether they like mammoth fresh or smelly. Fresh I think. Not everybody like smelly mammoth.
4:32 PM 12th Feb 65,982 BC from NetAnderthal

Cro-M01 One never knows what to take to these affairs. Could bring flowers but have horrid suspicion they'd eat them.
4:33 PM 12th Feb 65,982 BC from SapiensWeb

OG Okay, off to get dinner! Where my spear gone?
4:34 PM 12th Feb 65,982 BC from NetAnderthal

Cro-M01 We could gather some berries on the way over. I've always been quite good at gathering. Failed hunting miserably.
4:35 PM 12th Feb 65,982 BC from SapiensWeb

OG Og think that went quite well!
10:15 PM 12th Feb 65,982 BC from NetAnderthal

Cro-M01 OH MY SAINTED FUR BOOTS what a night.
10:16 PM 12th Feb 65,982 BC from SapiensWeb

OG Mr. And Mrs. Crowman VERY nice and so clean!
10:18 PM 12th Feb 65,982 BC from NetAnderthal

Cro-M01 He kept calling me "Mr. Crowman". It's CRO-MAGNON, with a hyphen. Of the Levant Cro-Magnons.
10:19 PM 12th Feb 65,982 BC from SapiensWeb

OG Mrs. Og make FRESHEST MAMMOTH EVER.
10:21 PM 12th Feb 65,982 BC from NetAnderthal

Cro-M01 You simply wouldn't believe what these oafs consider to be dinner. HAIRY ELEPHANT. A WHOLE HAIRY ELEPHANT.
10:23 PM 12th Feb 65,982 BC from SapiensWeb

OG Took ages to drag back to cave but worth it for look on Mr. Crowman face!
10:24 PM 12th Feb 65,982 BC from NetAnderthal

Cro-M01 When I suggested perhaps we ought to cook it they looked at me in UTTER bewilderment, poor souls. Tried to demonstrate.
10:27 PM 12th Feb 65,982 BC from SapiensWeb

OG Mr. Crowman do BRILLIANT TRICK with two sticks and bit of dry grass. Oooo!
10:29 PM 12th Feb 65,982 BC from NetAnderthal

Cro-M01 I get a paltry flame going and they start hooting and laughing and leaping about the place. Honestly, I didn't know where to look.
10:31 PM 12th Feb 65,982 BC from SapiensWeb

OG Og think us and Crowmans gonna be bestest friends EVER.
10:35 PM 12th Feb 65,982BC from NetAnderthal

Cro-M01 This isn't going to work at all. Either they or we will simply have to go.
10:36 PM 12th Feb 65,982 BC from SapiensWeb

#EARLIESTWRITING

Ug [cave writing symbols]
fireball high in sky 3rd May 35,000 BC from trogolodeck

Ig @Ug [cave writing symbols]
fireball high in sky 3rd May 35,000 BC from paleolithtwit

Ug @Ig [cave writing symbols]
fireball high in sky 3rd May 35,000 BC from trogolodeck

Ig @Ug [cave writing symbols]
fireball high in sky 3rd May 35,000 BC from paleolithtwit

Ug @Ig [cave writing symbols]
fireball high in sky 3rd May 35,000 BC from trogolodeck

Translation by Marcelino Sanz de Sautuola, Altimera, Spain, 1879

Ug I wonder of this kind of communication ever will take off.
fireball high in sky 3rd May 35,000 BC from trogolodeck

Ig @Ug I know. Just think. A way of expressing our thoughts and ideas with no boundaries or limits or rules.
fireball high in sky 3rd May 35,000 BC from paleolithtwit

Ug @Ig Actually I was thinking of restricting all cave paintings to 140 pictures or less.
fireball high in sky 3rd May 35,000 BC from trogolodeck

Ig @Ug That's a stupid idea.
fireball high in sky 3rd May 35,000 BC from paleolithtwit

Ug @Ig You say that now, but one day everyone will be doing it.
fireball high in sky 3rd May 35,000 BC from trogolodeck

#THEINVENTION OFTHEWHEEL

Atra-Hasis is making pots in his workshop in the city of Ur, as usual. Sigh.
3:32 PM 12th Apr 4732 BC from MesopotamiaNet

Atra-Hasis can't help but feel that there should be more to life than making pots in his workshop in the city of Ur. Ho-hum.
3:35 PM 12th Apr 4732 BC from MesopotamiaNet

Atra-Hasis is wondering if these "city" things will catch on. Lively but a bit rough and it doesn't smell too good when it's hot, which it usually is.
3:42 PM 12th Apr 4732 BC from MesopotamiaNet

Atra-Hasis is reflecting that at least making pots is a lot easier since @Ubara-Tutu invented this twirly thing to make them on.
3:45 PM 12th Apr 4732 BC from MesopotamiaNet

Atra-Hasis Whee!
3:46 PM 12th Apr 4732 BC from MesopotamiaNet

Atra-Hasis This bit used to take ages. Whee!
3:47 PM 12th Apr 4732 BC from MesopotamiaNet

Atra-Hasis has made ANOTHER POT and will put it on the the shelf with ALL THE OTHERS.
3:50 PM 12th Apr 4732 BC from MesopotamiaNet

Atra-Hasis Still, twirling the twirly thing is fun. Wheee!
3:54 PM 12th Apr 4732 BC from MesopotamiaNet

Atra-Hasis Hmmm...
3:55 PM 12th Apr 4732 BC from MesopotamiaNet

Atra-Hasis might be having an idea.
3:56 PM 12th Apr 4732 BC from MesopotamiaNet

Atra-Hasis is wondering if the twirly thing might
not have wider applications.
3:58 PM 12th Apr 4732 BC from MesopotamiaNet

Atra-Hasis is wondering what would happen if the twirly
thing were perpendicular to the ground, rather than parallel.
3:59 PM 12th Apr 4732 BC from MesopotamiaNet

Atra-Hasis thinks maybe if he were to lay the edge
of the twirly thing on the ground and push...
4:00 PM 12th Apr 4732 BC from MesopotamiaNet

Atra-Hasis is about to give it a go and will
be back in a minute.
4:02 PM 12th Apr 4732 BC from MesopotamiaNet

Atra-Hasis is now covered in wet clay, and realises this
was a silly idea.
4:10 PM 12th Apr 4732 BC from MesopotamiaNet

Atra-Hasis has turned the twirly thing the right way
up again and is making another pot.
4:15 PM 12th Apr 4732 BC from MesopotamiaNet

#CONSTRUCTIONOF THEPYRAMIDS

Hemon Monday morning meeting with the builders.
8:58 AM 3rd Jun 2540 BC from my nilePhone

Hemon Just heard that @Khufu wants some kind of big building constructing on the plateau at Giza.
8:58 AM 3rd Jun 2540 BC from my nilePhone

Hemon @vizierHenunu has just told him he'll never get planning permission.
9:05 AM 3rd Jun 2450 BC from my nilePhone

Hemon @vizierHenunu is dead.
9:06 AM 3rd Jun 2540 BC from my nilePhone

Hemon I'm keeping my mouth shut.
9:07 AM 3rd Jun 2540 BC from my nilePhone

Hemon Yes, he definitely wants a new build. Says it must be the biggest thing ever built and he wants it made of stone.
9:10 AM 3rd Jun 2540 BC from my nilePhone

Hemon A great big square building made of stone.
9:10 AM 3rd Jun 2540 BC from my nilePhone

Hemon Scratch that. A what??
9:11 AM 3rd Jun 2540 BC from my nilePhone

Hemon Oh for Horus's sake. He only wants a bloody pyramid.
9:11 AM 3rd Jun 2540 BC from my nilePhone

Hemon Such a pain in the arse. They're really hard to build.
@Snefru's was a right bastard.
9:13 AM 3rd Jun 2540 BC from my nilePhone

Hemon Couldn't get the angles right. Sides went all wonky.
9:13 AM 3rd Jun 2540 BC from my nilePhone

Hemon @Snefru's architect now killed of course.
9:14 AM 3rd Jun 2540 BC from my nilePhone

Hemon Oh God. Now he's got some plans out. He wants a tunnel
and a chamber and a secret trapdoor and a fake tunnel with a pit
at the end of it.
9:20 AM 3rd Jun 2540 BC from my nilePhone

Hemon Tsk. Doesn't want much does he? Why doesn't he just ask
for the pointy top to made of gold and be done with it??
9:22 AM 3rd Jun 2540 BC from my nilePhone

Hemon Damn.
9:25 AM 3rd Jun 2540 BC from my nilePhone

Hemon Just asked him what it's for, exactly.
9:27 AM 3rd Jun 2540 BC from my nilePhone

Hemon He says it's not really for anything. It's just an elaborate joke. Just wants to confuse future archaeologists.
9:28 AM 3rd Jun 2540 BC from my nilePhone

Hemon He's such a show off. More money than sense this bloke IMHO.
9:30 AM 3rd Jun 2540 BC from my nilePhone

IMHO @Hemon Hello? Somebody just give me a mention?
9:32 AM 3rd Jun 2540BC from phar02

Hemon @IMHO No, Imhotep, they didn't. Although I don't suppose you can lay our hands on 2.5 million individual enormous stone blocks at short notice?
9:33 AM 3rd Jun 2540 BC from my nilePhone

IMHO @Hemon nope, sorry. Too busy at the mo inventing Egyptian medicine and improving the quality of papyrus.
9:35 AM 3rd Jun 2540 BC from phar02

Hemon @IMHO OK. Anyway, just told him it's not the parts it's the labour. We can't start building the pyramids 'til next month.
9:36 AM 3rd Jun 2540 BC from my nilePhone

Hemon I'm having trouble finding any reliable alien builders from a technologically advanced planet.
9:36 AM 3rd Jun 2540 BC from my nilePhone

Hemon Think they've got another job on.
9:37 AM 3rd Jun 2540 BC from my nilePhone

Hemon Yep just checked. They've got another 3 weeks to go on Stonehenge.
9:43 AM 3rd Jun 2540 BC from my nilePhone

Hemon *sigh*
9:43 AM 3rd Jun 2540 BC from my nilePhone

#STONEHENGE

Uthbad1 Guys, guys, they're just putting the last lintel in place. You gotta see this. #hengecompletion
3:46 PM 4th May 1929 BC from RowanBerry

mulg @Uthbad1 How's it looking man? #hengecompletion
3:47 PM 4th May 1929 BC from DruidNet

Uthbad1 @mulg It's amazing! Seriously, people are going to be looking at this in like DOZENS of years time. #hengecompletion
3:48 PM 4th May 1929 BC from RowanBerry

mulg @Uthbad1 Never mind that, is it like gonna WORK. #hengecompletion
3:50 PM 4th May 1929 BC from DruidNet

Uthbad1 @mulg well we won't know that till the solstice will we. #hengecompletion
3:51 PM 4th May 1929 BC from RowanBerry

mulg @Uthbad1 Right. Heavy. See you there then I suppose. #hengecompletion
3:52 PM 4th May 1929 BC from DruidNet

Uthbad1 #hengeday Is everybody here?
4:09 AM 21st Jun 1929 BC from RowanBerry

mulg #hengeday I'm over by the Northern triptych. Look I'm waving.
4:10 AM 21st Jun 1929 BC from DruidNet

Uthbad1 #hengeday It's completely dark and I'm about a hundred yards away, I can't see you.
4:11 AM 21st Jun 1929 BC from RowanBerry

mulg #hengeday I'm waving my torch. Does that help?
4:12 AM 21st Jun 1929 BC from DruidNet

Uthbad1 #hengeday Not really. Everyone's waving torches. All I can see is hundreds of waving torches.
4:13 AM 21st Jun 1929 BC from RowanBerry

mulg #hengeday I'm waving it REALLY FAST.
4:14 AM 21st Jun 1929 BC from DruitNet

mulg #hengeday Bugger, my torch went out.
4.15 AM 21st Jun 1929 BC from DruidNet

Uthbad1 #hengeday It doesn't matter. Where's @Drogln?
4:16 AM 21st Jun 1929 BC from RowanBerry

Drogln #hengeday I'm here but I just smashed my nose on a big stone something. Ow.
4:17 AM 21st Jun 1929 BC from MistletoeMobile

Uthbad1 #hengeday roflmao! Drogln you stoned entrail-head, watch where you're walking man.
4:18 AM 21st Jun 1929 BC from RowanBerry

Drogln That really hurt guys, not funny. #hengeday
4:19 AM 21st Jun 1929 BC from MistletoeMobile

Uthbad1 @mulg OMGs PMSL! Drogln just walked right into it! #hengeday
4:20 AM 21st Jun 1929 BC from RowanBerry

Drogln Seriously drudes I think my nose is broken :(#hengeday
4:21 AM 21st Jun 1929 BC from MistletoeMobile

mulg @Drogln How the hell do you not see the biggest stone circle in all Tir Nan Og? #hengeday
4:22 AM 21st Jun 1929 BC from DruidNet

Drogln @mulg It's not my fault man, it's totally dark out here! Why did we have to meet in the middle of the night? #hengeday
4:23 AM 21st Jun 1929 BC from MistletoeMobile

Uthbad1 @Drogln Because we have to be here when the sun comes up, you stupid goat botherer #hengeday
4:24 AM 21st Jun 1929 BC from RowanBerry

mulg @Drogln Why didn't you bring a torch like everyone else? #hengeday
4:25 AM 21st Jun 1929 BC from DruidNet

Drogln @mulg Hey man, fire gives off like negative vibes, everyone knows that #hengeday
4:26 AM 21st Jun 1929 BC from MistletoeMobile

Uthbad1 Hey quiet everyone! Look, the sun's coming up! #hengeday
4.27 AM 21st Jun 1929 BC from RowanBerry

mulg @Uthbad1 @Drogln here we go guys #hengeday
4:28 AM 21st Jun 1929 BC from DruidNet

Uthbad1 Here it comes #hengeday
4:29 AM 21st Jun 1929 BC from RowanBerry

Uthbad1 Still coming #hengeday
4:31 AM 21st Jun 1929 BC from RowanBerry

Uthbad1 Any minute now #hengeday
4:33 AM 21st Jun 1929 BC from RowanBerry

Drogln Has anyone got any nuts? #hengeday
4:34 AM 21st Jun 1929 BC from MistletoeMobile

mulg @drogln Sh! #hengeday
4:35 AM 21st Jun 1929 BC from DruidNet

Drogln I'm hungry #hengeday
4:3 AM 21st Jun 1929 BC from MistletoeMobile

Uthbad1 Look! It's happening! The sun's rising exactly between
the uprights of the Eastern trilithon! #hengeday
4:37 AM 21st Jun 1929 BC from RowanBerry

mulg It works! It only bloody works! #hengeday
4:38 AM 21st Jun 1929 BC from DruidNet

Uthbad1 Woo! #hengewin
4:38 AM 21st Jun 1929 BC from RowanBerry

Drogln Or some acorns? Bit of bark, anything, I'm starving
#hengeday
4:38 AM 21st Jun 1929 BC from MistletoeMobile

Uthbad1 This means we, the druids, have constructed a perfectly
accurate calendric clock! #hengewin
4:39 AM 21st Jun 1929 BC from RowanBerry

mulg We can now tell exactly what time of day it is on what day of
the year! Woo hoo! #hengewin
4:40 AM 21st Jun 1929 BC from DruidNet

Drogln As long as we're standing in this field. #hengeday
4:41 AM 21st Jun 1929 BC from MistletoeMobile

Uthbad1 @Drogln What?
4:41 AM 21st Jun 1929 BC from RowanBerry

Drogln We can tell what time it is and what day it is as long as
we're standing in this part of this field. #hengeday
4:42 AM 21st Jun 1929 BC from MistletoeMobile

mulg Oh. #hengeday
4:43 AM 21st Jun 1929 BC from DruidNet

Uthbad1 Bummer. #hengeday
4:44 AM 21st Jun 1929 BC from RowanBerry

Drogln I said they were making it too big. I'd have made a little
one you could carry about. #hengeday
4:45 AM 21st Jun 1929BC from MistletoeMobile

Drogln Oh far out, I found some mushrooms. #hengeday
4:46 AM 21st Jun 1929 BC from MistletoeMobile

#TROY

Stavros This is ridiculous. They are NEVER going to go for this. #horsescam
8:05 AM 7th Jul 1250 BC from GreekBerry

Christos Why did we come here in the first place? Remind me. #horsescam
8:06 AM 7th Jul 1250 BC from mycenaePhone

Stavros The story I got was that we've come to get Menelaus's bird back but that can't be it, surely. A thousand ships for one bird? #horsescam
8:07 AM 7th Jul 1250 BC from GreekBerry

Stavros Didn't know we HAD a thousand ships #horsescam
8:08 AM 7th Jul 1250 BC from mycenaePhone

Christos I mean I was on ship no. 983 so the story's bound to have got a bit diluted by the time it got to us. #horsescam
8:09 AM 7th Jul 1250 BC from GreekBerry

Stavros Still seems pretty unlikely. All this for a chick. You're a king, Menelaus, just get a new one. Chicks dig kings. #horsescam
8:11 AM 7th Jul 1250 BC from mycenaePhone

Christos Absolutely. If Ajax can get laid with that face it shouldn't be too hard for someone with an actual kingdom and everything. #horsescam
8:11 AM 7th Jul 1250 BC from GreekBerry

Stavros So how long do we have to stay in here? Can't bloody breathe. #horsescam
8:12 AM 7th Jul 1250 BC from mycenaePhone

Christos Until Aggie realises this is the stupidest idea he's ever had, I suppose. #horsescam
8:12 AM 7th Jul 1250 BC from GreekBerry

Stavros If you can't climb the walls or smash the walls, they win, it's over, go home. Them's the rules. #horsescam
8:13 AM 7th Jul 1250 BC from mycenaePhone

Christos Was it Odysseus who said "wait, don't these guys have a thing about horses?" I'd like to kick his arse. #horsescam
8:15 AM 7th Jul 1250 BC from GreekBerry

Stavros Next thing you know, we're up two nights hammering and chiselling. #horsescam
8:16 AM 7th Jul 1250 BC from mycenaePhone

Christos And now I'm crammed into this absurd contraption with my face wedged up against Achilles's admittedly magnificent buttcheeks. #horsescam
8:17 AM 7th Jul 1250 BC from GreekBerry

Stavros Nobody is dumb enough to wheel a horse-shaped crate full of Greeks trying not to giggle into their city. #horsescam
8:18 AM 7th Jul 1250 BC from mycenaePhone

Christos Seriously though, they are superb. D'you think he waxes them or are they naturally this smooth? #horsescam
8:18 AM 7th Jul 1250 BC from GreekBerry

Stavros Hang on a minute... #horsescam
8:19 AM 7th Jul 1250 BC from mycenaePhone

Christos I'm gonna try and get his autograph before they open this thing up. #horsescam
8:20 AM 7th Jul 1250 BC from GreekBerry

Stavros Don't touch his feet. He's weird about his feet. Do you hear something? #horsescam
8:20 AM 7th Jul 1250 BC from mycenaePhone

Paris1 @Helenbabes Oh look, darling, they've left us a present. How terribly sweet and magnanimous.
8:20 AM 7th Jul 1250 BC from TroyDeck

Helenbabes @Paris1 Well, you know the old saying, "Greeks do give the nicest gifts".
8:21 AM 7th Jul 1250 BC from TroyDeck

Paris1 @Helenbabes How true. I'll see if I can get some strapping young chaps to give me a hand bringing it in. Toodle oo sweetums.
8:22 AM 7th Jul 1250 BC from TroyDeck

Helenbabes @Paris1 Bysie bye angel cakes.
8:23 AM 7th Jul 1250 BC from TroyDeck

Stavros #horsescam I don't bloody believe it.
8:24 AM 7th Jul 1250 BC from mycenaePhone

Achilles #horsescam Prepare to die for the glory of Greece, my brothers, and whoever that is back there STOP NUZZLING.
8:24 AM 7th Jul 1250 BC from MyrmidonLine

#CERNE ABBAS

CerneAbbasDave Oi! I spent weeks carving that giant into the hillside, now which one of you bastards drew THAT THING on it?!
8:18 AM 21st Jun 606 BC from PaganBerry

satrap @Cyrus Morning!
9:12 AM 4th May 462 BC from AchaemenidWeb

Cyrus @satrap Yes, and what a beautiful morning it is that the God Emperor Xerxes has caused to happen by his word.
9:13 AM 4th May 462 BC from PersepolisPhone

satrap @Cyrus It certainly is. How lucky we are that The Great God Emperor Xerxes blesses us so rather than destroy us, as is in his power to do.
9:14 AM 4th May 462 BC from AchaemenidWeb

DIRECT MESSAGE FROM @Cyrus TO @satrap
Bollocks, I forgot to put GREAT God Emperor. Think he'll notice? They say he reads all of this.
9:15 AM 4th May 462 BC

DIRECT MESSAGE FROM @satrap TO @Cyrus Too bloody late now either way. Keep going.
9:16 AM 4th May 462 BC

Cyrus @satrap I was only saying to my wife "Parmys darling, how do you think The Great God Emperor Xerxes stays so wise and perfect?"
9:17 AM 4th May 462 BC from PersepolisPhone

DIRECT MESSAGE FROM @Cyrus TO @satrap Is there
an acceptable abbreviation for Great God Emperor?
Only it's eating up my character limit.
9:18 AM 4th May 462 BC

DIRECT MESSAGE FROM @satrap TO @Cyrus
You must be bloody joking.
9:19 AM 4th May 462 BC

satrap @Cyrus And what did she say?
9:20 AM 4th May 462 BC from AchaemenidWeb

Cyrus @satrap She said "Oh Cyrus, the ways of the sage and
beautiful Great God Emperor Xerxes are not for us to fathom".
9:21 AM 4th May 462 BC from PersepolisPhone

DIRECT MESSAGE FROM @satrap TO @Cyrus
"sage and beautiful" – easy, don't want to suck up too much.
9:22 AM 4th May 462 BC

DIRECT MESSAGE FROM @Cyrus TO @satrap
This is Xerxes we're talking about, there IS no "sucking up too
much". There may not even be a "sucking up enough".
9:23 AM 4th May 462 BC

satrap @Cyrus So, how can we best honour and venerate the Great
God Emperor Xerxes today then?
9:24 AM 4th May 462 BC from AchaemenidWeb

Cyrus @satrap I thought perhaps a couple of votive libations would
do the trick.
9:25 AM 4th May 462 BC from PersepolisPhone

DIRECT MESSAGE FROM @satrap TO @Cyrus
If that means "do you fancy a drink", then HELL yes.
9:26 AM 4th May 462 BC

#EASTERISLAND

Tu'u-kho Oh no, this one doesn't work EITHER.
1:12 PM 4th Jun 432 BC from RapaNuiOL

Tu'u-kho The chin sticks out too far and the nose is all wrong!
1:13 PM 4th Jun 432 BC from RapaNuiOL

Tu'u-kho And look at that massive forehead – FFS,
what was I thinking.
1:14 PM 4th Jun 432 BC from RapaNuiOL

Tu'u-kho It looks nothing like her! She's going to HATE it.
1:15 PM 4th Jun 432 BC from RapaNuiOL

Tu'u-kho I'll do another one.
1:17 PM 4th Jun 432 BC from RapaNuiOL

#ARCHIMEDES

MrsA REALLY need the lav but he's been in there for ages.
5:12 PM 20th May 245 BC from SyracuseWeb

MrsA Knocked on the door. Said "how much longer are you going to be in there?"
5:20 PM 20th May 245 BC from SyracuseWeb

MrsA He said, "Go away, I'm having an epiphany" I said "I've never heard it called that before."
5:22 PM 20th May 245 BC from SyracuseWeb

MrsA He's just come running out stark naked and soaking wet. He looked at me, shouted "you reeker!" and ran off into the street.
5:33 PM 20th May 245 BC from SyracuseWeb

MrsA I shouted after him "if I'm a reeker it's because you've used all the bloody hot water again" but he was already halfway down the street.
5:35 PM 20th May 245 BC from SyracuseWeb

MrsA He'll be back when he wants his dinner or notices he's naked. He gets so distracted when he's got a theorem on the go.
5:38 PM 20th May 245 BC from SyracuseWeb

#HANNIBAL CROSSESTHEALPS

Hannibal So, everyone set for the march into Italy tomorrow?
5:34 PM 23rd Mar 218 BC from MrCarthage

hasdrubalthefair @hannibal What's the route? Presumably following the coast of France down below the Pyrenees and then go round to avoid the Alps?
5:35 PM 23rd Mar 218 BC from MrCarthage

Hannibal @hasdrubalthefair Nah. I thought we'd go over the Pyrenees and then over the Alps.
5:36 PM 23rd Mar 218 BC from MrCarthage

Hannibal @hasdrubalthefair Otherwise it'll take weeks...
5:37 PM 23rd Mar 218 BC from MrCarthage

hasdrubalthefair @hannibal Yes but in case it'd escaped ur attention we've got a f**kload of elephants. How exactly do you propose to get them up a mountain?
5:38 PM 23rd Mar 218 BC from MrCarthage

Hannibal @hasdrubalthefair Oh ye of little faith. They'll be fine.
5:39 PM 23rd Mar 218 BC from MrCarthage

hasdrubalthefair @hannibal They won't be fine. They weigh about 26000lbs each and are 14 feet high. I'm not pulling them up.
5:40 PM 23rd Mar 218 BC from MrCarthage

hasdrubalthefair @hannibal Not only that, but given that elephants are indigenous to a hot climate .....
5:41 PM 23rd Mar 218 BC from MrCarthage

hasdrubalthefair @hannibal … can I ask how do you expect them to cope with the kinds of temperatures that you get up an alp?
5:41 PM 23rd Mar 218 BC from MrCarthage

Hannibal @hasdrubalthefair Chill out, dude. It's not gonna be a prob
5:42 PM 23rd Mar 218 BC from MrCarthage

hasdrubalthefair @hannibal It's not me chilling out you need to be worried about, it's the elephants.
5:43 PM 23rd Mar 218 BC from MrCarthage

Hannibal @hasdrubalthefair Look, quite simply we'll build a road for them as we go.
5:45 PM 23rd Mar 218 BC from MrCarthage

hasdrubalthefair @hannibal WHAT?? You don't think it's enough that we'll be taking 40,000 foot soldiers and 12,000 horsemen mountain climbing?
5:47 PM 23rd Mar 218 BC from MrCarthage

hasdrubalthefair @hannibal And what about food? Have you any idea how much an elephant eats on a daily basis?
5:48 PM 23rd Mar 218 BC from MrCarthage

hasdrubalthefair @hannibal I'm rapidly coming to the conclusion that you know f**k all about elephants.
5:50 PM 23rd Mar 218 BC from MrCarthage

Hannibal @hasdrubalthefair Fine. Forget the elephants. We'll take gibbons. F**king war gibbons. Happy now?
5:53 PM 23rd Mar 218 BC from MrCarthage

hasdrubalthefair @hannibal Twat.
5:54 PM 23rd Mar 218 BC from MrCarthage

Hannibal @hasdrubalthefair Dickhead.
5:54 PM 23rd Mar 218 BC from MrCarthage

#THEDEATHOF JULIUSCAESAR

Caesar Just signed up to this.
10:20 AM 15th Mar 44 BC from SPQRnet

Caesar is wondering what to write.
10:25 AM 15th Mar 44 BC from SPQRnet

Caesar I don't really get this. What do I do?
10:32 AM 15th Mar 44 BC from SPQRnet

Brutus @caesar has joined. Let's make him welcome.
10:33 AM 15th Mar 44 BC from romeingmobile

Caesar Hi Brutus. Hi everyone.
10:34 AM 15th Mar 44 BC from SPQRnet

Brutus pic of me and @Caesar with our thumbs up inside
the coliseum. http://tinyurl.com/23s9tp
10:36 AM 15th Mar 44 BC from romeingmobile

Brutus @Caesar Don't forget the meeting at the Senate tonight.
10:37 AM 15th Mar 44 BC from SPQRnet

Caesar @Brutus Will you be there?
10:38 AM 15th Mar 44 BC from SPQRnet

Brutus @Caesar Oh yes. Me and all the others. @casca @tillius
@gaiscassiuslonginus and the guys.
10:39 AM 15th Mar 44 BC from SPQRnet

Caesar @Brutus all of them? Why?
What's so special about tonight?
10:41 AM 15th Mar 44 BC from SPQRnet

Brutus @Caesar Not saying! Bit of a surprise for you!
10:44 AM 15th Mar 44 BC from SPQRnet

Caesar RT @soothsayer just sent me this: #bewaretheidesofmarch
What does that mean?
10:47 AM 15th Mar 44 BC from SPQRnet

Brutus Don't worry about it.
10:48 AM 15th Mar 44 BC from SPQRnet

Caesar @Brutus Gotta go. About to enter Forum and
the signal's shite.
10:51 AM 15th Mar 44 BC from SPQRnet

Brutus @Caesar What network are you on?
10:51 AM 15th Mar 44 BC from SPQRnet

Caesar @Brutus O2 Brute.
10:51 AM 15th Mar 44 BC from SPQRnet

gaiuscassiuslonginus @Brutus Has @Caesar logged off?
11:01 AM 15th Mar 44 BC from remustweet

Brutus @gaiuscassiuslonginus Yes.
11:01 AM 15th Mar 44 BC from SPQRnet

gaiuscassiuslonginus @Brutus Good. Bloke's a tosser.
11:02 AM 15th Mar 44 BC from remustweet

#MARYANDJOSEPH

joseph @mary just finishing off a simple rudimentary table then leaving work. Reckon we'll be on the road by 6.
4:38 PM 18th Dec 6 BC from my NazBerry

mary @joseph how long will it take to get there?
4:39 PM 18th Dec 6 BC from virginmobile

joseph @mary I reckon about a week depending on traffic.
4:39 PM 18th Dec 6 BC from My NazBerry

mary @joseph did you remember to book the hotel?
4:40 PM 18th Dec 6 BC from virginmobile

joseph @mary of course. Got a bargain on www.lateinns.com
4:41 PM 18th Dec 6 BC from My NazBerry

mary @joseph only I don't want to be hunting for one when we get there. Not in my condition.
4:41 PM 18th Dec 6 BC from virginmobile

joseph @mary have you fed the donkey?
4:42 PM 18th Dec 6 BC from My NazBerry

mary @joseph yes.
4:43 PM 18th Dec 6 BC from virginmobile

joseph @mary only it'll need to keep it's strength up.
4:44 PM 18th Dec 6 BC from My NazBerry

mary @joseph is this about my size?
4:45 PM 18th Dec 6 BC from virginmobile

joseph @mary eh? no.
4:45 PM 18th Dec 6 BC from My NazBerry

mary @joseph seriously, are you saying I'm too heavy for a donkey?
4:45 PM 18th Dec 6 BC from virginmobile

joseph @mary Jesus Christ. No!
4:45 PM 18th Dec 6 BC from My NazBerry

mary @joseph because it's not my fault I'm up the stick is it?
4:46 PM 18th Dec 6 BC from virginmobile

joseph @mary well it's not f**king mine!
4:46 PM 18th Dec 6 BC from My NazBerry

mary @joseph oh here we go again.
4:47 PM 18th Dec 6 BC from virginmobile

joseph @mary well all I'm saying is that it's a bit suspicious.
4:48 PM 18th Dec 6 BC from My NazBerry

mary @joseph so you keep saying and I keep telling you it's a miracle of the Lord.
4:49 PM 18th Dec 6 BC from virginmobile

joseph @mary so why cant we have a DNA test?
4.50 PM 18th Dec 6BC from My NazBerry

mary @joseph not this again.
4:51 PM 18th Dec 6 BC from virginmobile

joseph @mary I'm just saying it's all a bit convenient.
4:52 PM 18th Dec 6 BC from My NazBerry

mary @joseph look. I've told you what happened a dozen times. The holy ghost came down and touched me and made me with child.
4:53 PM 18th Dec 6 BC from virginmobile

joseph @mary While I was at work?
4:54 PM 18th Dec 6 BC from My NazBerry

mary @joseph Yes, like I told you, yes.
4:54 PM 18th Dec 6 BC from virginmobile

joseph @mary But I've only got your word for it haven't I?
4:55 PM 18th Dec 6 BC from My NazBerry

mary @joseph how many times are we going to go through this?
4:56 PM 18th Dec 6 BC from virginmobile

joseph @mary I just think this whole immaculate conception thing is a bit weird that's all. It's all just a bit hard to swallow.
4:57 PM 18th Dec 6 BC from My NazBerry

joseph @mary I mean it's never happened before or since has it, so why us?
4:57 PM 18th Dec 6 BC from My NazBerry

mary @joseph I guess because we're touched by God.
4:58 PM 18th Dec 6 BC from virginmobile

joseph @mary well I guess someone was. While someone else was at work.
4:58 PM 18th Dec 6 BC from My NazBerry

mary @joseph I'm not having this conversation. We've got a long journey tonight so can you just drop it?
4:59 PM 18th Dec 6 BC from virginmobile

joseph @mary Whatever.
5:01 PM 18th Dec 6 BC from My NazBerry

DIRECT MESSAGE FROM @angelgabriel @mary Hiya babes. How
u? Does your old man suspect anything?
5:05 PM 18th Dec 6 BC from heavenlyhosting

DIRECT MESSAGE FROM @mary @angelgabriel Nope. Still going
with the whole immaculate conception thing.
5:05 PM 18th Dec 6 BC from virginmobile

DIRECT MESSAGE FROM @angelgabriel @mary Nice one. Cool.
5:06 PM 18th Dec 6 BC from heavenlyhosting

DIRECT MESSAGE FROM @mary @angelgabriel L8trs babe.
5:06 PM 18th Dec 6 BC from heavenlyhosting

DIRECT MESSAGE FROM @angelgabriel @mary Don't b a stranger.
5:07 PM 18th Dec 6 BC from virginmobile

joseph @mary www.lateinns.com just sent a message.
They've cocked up the booking and they're full.
5:12 PM 18th Dec 6 BC from My NazBerry

mary @joseph Oh for God's sake. Can't you get anything right?
5:13 PM 18th Dec 6 BC from virginmobile

#EASTER

GOOD FRIDAY

jesushchrist well what a crap day this is turning out to be.
2:35 PM 3rd Apr AD 33 from crucifixfon

jesushchrist Have to stop tweeting in a mo. Need both hands to use phone and that's just not going to be happening.
2:37 PM 3rd Apr AD 33 from crucifixfon

jesushchrist @God why have you forsaken me?
2:39 PM 3rd Apr AD 33 from crucifixfon

jesushchrist RT @God out of office reply.
2:40 PM 3rd Apr AD 33 from crucifixfon

EASTER SATURDAY

judasiscariot1 Am 30 quid up but feel terrible.
10:27 AM 4th Apr AD 33 from fishermansNet

jesushchrist @judasiscariot1 Don't sweat it. Just came back to life. Clearly crucifixion not as bad as they make it out to be.
11:05 AM 4th Apr AD 33 from crucifixfon

jesushchrist Stuck in tomb though. Hoping to get out tomorrow. Am drawing on shroud in permanent marker pen to pass the time.
11:07 AM 4th Apr AD 33 from crucifixfon

EASTER SUNDAY

prozziemary just arrived at tomb to find stone rolled away. WTF??
9:03 AM 5th Apr AD 33 from apostleweb

prozziemary No-one round here seems to know anything about
it. There must have been a handle on the inside.
9:11 AM 5th Apr AD 33 from apostleweb

thomas @prozziemary doubt it.
9:14 AM 5th Apr AD 33 from fishermansNet

jesushchrist @prozziemary Nope, @thomas is right. @God finally
came through and let me out. Apologised. Apparently he'd been
away for the Easter break.
9:21 AM 5th Apr AD 33 from crucifixfon

45

#THEDISCOVERY
OFTHEAMERICAS

LiefSonOfEric Where the f**k are we?
8:15 AM 12th Mar 1002 from ThorMobile

LiefSonOfEric No seriously, where the f**k are we?
8:17 AM 12th Mar 1002 from ThorMobile

LiefSonOfEric Does anybody remember ANYTHING from last night?
8:20 AM 12th Mar 1002 from ThorMobile

LiefSonOfEric Last I can recall we'd all had a skinful and Rorik Son Of Rorik Rorikson challenged me to a longboat race. Guess I accepted.
8:22 AM 12th Mar 1002 from ThorMobile

LiefSonOfEric Then Ingvar The Irresponsible shouts "Last one off the edge of the world is a poof" there was a big cheer and after that it's all a blur.
8:23 AM 12th Mar 1002 from ThorMobile

LiefSonOfEric Odin's balls, my head's killing me.
8:45 AM 12th Mar 1002 from ThorMobile

LiefSonOfEric I wouldn't mind but there's bugger all to rape or pillage here. Not so much as a bloody goat.
8:48 AM 12th Mar 1002 from ThorMobile

LiefSonOfEric Not that I ever have.
8:50 AM 12th Mar 1002 from ThorMobile

LiefSonOfEric Well there was that one time at Ragnar's birthday party. A bet's a bet.
8:51 AM 12th Mar 1002 from ThorMobile

LiefSonOfEric So what are we going to call this place? Suggestions?
12:32 PM 12th Mar 1002 from ThorMobile

LiefSonOfEric Well it's a land, it's new and we found it. Hmm.
12:36 PM 12th Mar 1002 from ThorMobile

LiefSonOfEric Landfoundnew?
1:04 PM 12th Mar 1002 from ThorMobile

LiefSonOfEric Newlandfound?
2:11 PM 12th Mar 1002 from ThorMobile

LiefSonOfEric Got it! Nova Scotia! No idea what it means but it's got a ring to it. Right, well if we're staying for a bit we may as well get comfy.
9:23 AM 13th Mar 1002 from ThorMobile

LiefSonOfEric That banqueting table Thorvald made has collapsed AGAIN. And Orvik's chairs are all wonky.
4:02 PM 15th Apr 1002 from ThorMobile

LiefSonOfEric Guys, we HAVE to think of some way to make it easier to build furniture.
4:05 PM 15th Apr 1002 from ThorMobile

#THEBATTLE OFHASTINGS

KingHarold leading men into battle against the Normans. French. 7,500 of us, 8,400 of them. Should be a piece of piss.
3:55 PM 13th Oct 1066 from SaxonNet

KingHarold Oh and there's some tapestry people following me around embroidering a documentary.
4:02 PM 13th Oct 1066 from SaxonNet

KingHarold They say its an objective and highly acclaimed look behind the scenes at the disputed succession to the throne of England.
4:05 PM 13th Oct 1066 from SaxonNet

KingHarold The documentary guys have given me a sneak preview of the days stitches – reckon I'm coming across pretty well! www.twitpic.com/bayeaux
6:13 PM 13th Oct 1066 from SaxonNet

KingHarold Tomorrow we're at Senlac Hill just outside Hastings for a scrap with the French and the director has had an idea!
6:17 PM 13th Oct 1066 from SaxonNet

KingHarold Says he'll tell me what it is tomorrow when he sets up the tableau! Ace! Nite all.
6:20 PM 13th Oct 1066 from SaxonNet

KingHarold Morning all! Director wants me to pose with chin up gazing into the sky as the enemy fire their arrows at us into the sky!
10:04 AM 14th Oct 1066 from SaxonNet

KingHarold This is going to look so cool on the tapestry.
10:10 AM 14th Oct 1066 from SaxonNet

KingHarold Ow. F**k.
10:11 AM 14th Oct 1066 from SaxonNet

#GENGHISKHANAND
THEMONGOLHORDES

Genghis @generalsubutai How's it going?
11:17 AM 3rd Nov 1218 from empireWeb

generalsubutai @Genghis Fine. Although there's a problem with the hordes.
11:18 AM 3rd Nov 1218 from dynastweet

Genghis @generalsubutai What problem?
11:19 AM 3rd Nov 1218 from empireWeb

generalsubutai @Genghis it's the name. The name of the hordes.
11:21 AM 3rd Nov 1218 from dynastweet

Genghis @generalsubutai What about the name of the hordes?
11:22 AM 3rd Nov 1218 from empireWeb

generalsubutai @Genghis Well, it's not very PC is it?
11:23 AM 3rd Nov 1218 from dynastweet

Genghis @generalsubutai What do you mean?
11:24 AM 3rd Nov 1218 from empireWeb

generalsubutai @Genghis Well it's just that times have changed and that word is no longer very politically correct.
11:25 AM 3rd Nov 1218 from dynastweet

Genghis @generalsubutai What word?
11:26 AM 3rd Nov 1218 from empireWeb

generalsubutai @Genghis THE word. You know, the 'M' word. Don't make me tweet it.
11:27 AM 3rd Nov 1218 from dynastweet

Genghis @generalsubutai Oh for heaven's sake.
11:28 AM 3rd Nov 1218 from empireWeb

generalsubutai @Genghis I'm afraid what was acceptable 2 years ago in 1216 just isn't acceptable any more.
11:28 AM 3rd Nov 1218 from dynastweet

Genghis @generalsubutai Oh for heaven's sake you can't say anything nowadays.
11:29 AM 3rd Nov 1218 from empireWeb

Genghis @generalsubutai Next you'll be telling me I can't hack someone's head apart and rip their limbs off 'cos it's a breach of health and safety.
11:31 AM 3rd Nov 1218 from empireWeb

Genghis @generalsubutai It's political correctness gone mad.
11:31 AM 3rd Nov 1218 from empireWeb

generalsubutai @Genghis Tell me about it. I've just come from back from one of our campaigns in Chinkyland and it's the same there.
11:32 AM 3rd Nov 1218 from dynastweet

Genghis @generalsubutai Honestly, I've had it with these bloody liberal do-gooders. This country's going to hell in a bronzed war chariot.
11:33 AM 3rd Nov 1218 from empireWeb

#ROBINHOOD
ANDHISMERRYMEN

robinhood just stopped a coach on way to Nottingham and
robbed a load of gold. Yay.
2:15 PM 14th May 1193 from b0w2

friartuck @robinhood get any food?
2:15 PM 14th May 1193 from monkmobile

robinhood @friartuck Do you ever think about anything other
than your stomach??
2:16 PM 14th May 1193 from b0w2

friartuck @robinhood yes well it's all very well nicking gold, Robin
but what about lunch?
2:17 PM 14th May 1193 from monkmobile

robinhood @friartuck what about the poor? I'm trying to do
the right thing here.
2:18 PM 14th May 1193 from b0w2

robinhood RT @littlejohn tuck's a big fat bastard, la la la la.
2:20 PM 14th May 1193 from b0w2

robinhood @littlejohn LOL.
2:20 PM 14th May 1193 from b0w2

robinhood RT @littlejohn I've always thought it ironic that if you
spoonerise 'Friar Tuck' you get something he's too fat to ever do.
2:22 PM 14th May 1193 from b0w2

friartuck @littlejohn you're a fine one to talk about irony. I mean *Little* John?? You're the size of a dung heap. You look like a dung heap in gay tights.
2:23 PM 14th May 1193 from monkmobile

robinhood Haha. ROFL
2:24 PM 14th May 1193 from b0w2

littlejohn @robinhood you can shut up as well. @friartuck's right. You're bloody obsessed with the poor. What ARE we having for lunch?
2:26 PM 14th May 1193 from tweetstaff

robinhood look taxes are high so I'm redistributing the wealth.
2:27 PM 14th May 1193 from b0w2

littlejohn @robinhood Your problem is that you've got no grasp of a capitalist free market economy.
2:28 PM 14th May 1193 from tweetstaff

friartuck @robinhood @littlejohn is right. This kind of amateur proto-socialism is a neo Marxist dream that's destined to fail.
2:29 PM 14th May 1193 from monkmobile

robinhood @friartuck shut up fatso.
2:34 PM 14th May 1193 from b0w2

friartuck @robinhood good comeback NOT. That took you five minutes to think of did it?
2:34 PM 14th May 1193 from monkmobile

alanadale hey everyone. Just joined twitter. Anyone want to hear my new song? It's a madrigal with a folk twist. www.myspace.com/alanadale
2:34 PM 14th May 1193 from lutetwit

robinhood RT @willscarlett @littlejohn @friartuck @muchthemillersson @maidmarian1 @nasirfromrobinofsherwood @sherrifofnottingham @gisburneguy NO! F**k off.
2:35 PM 14th May 1193 from b0w2

 **#THEBLACKDEATH**

BertWheeler So what are they saying now then? #plague
1:12 PM 4th Aug 1349 from PeasantNet

BertCooper Apparently it's the rats. Rats have got it and they're giving it to us. #plague
1:13 PM 4th Aug 1349 from WebSerf

BertMiller So I suppose we're not supposed to eat rats any more then? #plague
1:15 PM 4th Aug 1349 from Turnip

BertCooper I don't think eating them's the problem, I heard you're supposed to avoid contact with them. #plague
1:16 PM 4th Aug 1349 from WebSerf

BertMiller How are you supposed to eat them AND avoid contact with them? I don't get it. #plague
1:17 PM 4th Aug 1349 from Turnip

BertWheeler I know. That's the trouble with these public health warnings, they're so inconsistent. #plague
1:19 PM 4th Aug 1349 from PeasantNet

BertCooper It's like when they suddenly decided eating dung's bad for you. My dad ate dung every day of his life & he lived to be TWENTY EIGHT. #plague
1:21 PM 4th Aug 1349 from WebSerf

BertMiller People are so bloody lily-livered nowadays. All it takes is for half the population to die in agony and they fly into a mad panic. #plague
1:23 PM 4th Aug 1349 from Turnip

BertWheeler So what ARE we supposed to do? Apart from "avoid rats", like that's even an option. #plague
1:25 PM 4th Aug 1349 from PeasantNet

BertCooper Dunno. Pray lots? #plague
1:27 PM 4th Aug 1349 from WebSerf

BertMiller Well I say we should stick to burning Jews. Burning Jews were good enough in the old days and it's good enough now. #plague
1:29 PM 4th Aug 1349 from Turnip

BertWheeler Aye. Keep your new-fangled potions and remedies, you know where you are with burning Jews. #plague
1:31 PM 4th Aug 1349 from PeasantNet

#THEBATTLE OFAGINCOURT

Henry05 New blog entry up; draft of pre-battle pep talk for tomorrow: http://tinyurl.com/lfzfb9 Thoughts anybody? #agincourt
8:42 PM 24th Oct 1415 from PlantageNet

EXETER @Henry05 I like the "we happy few" bit but not sure about "band of brothers", sire. That sort of talk leads to succession quibbles.
8:43 PM 24th Oct 1415 from EarlPhone

BEDFORD @Henry05 I got a name check! Nice one my liege.
8:44 PM 24th Oct 1415 from DukeWeb

TALBOT @Henry05 Oh tits, is it St. Crispin's Day TOMORROW? Clean forgotten.
8:45 PM 24th Oct 1415 from LongBowMobile

EXETER @Henry05 And that bit about stripping your sleeve & showing your wounds – I don't actually intend GETTING wounded. That's what serfs are for.
8:46 PM 24th Oct 1415 from EarlPhone

CrazyJohnnyFalstaff @Henry05 Oh SOD the battle and come out on the lash! Got a couple of hot Welsh birds who are just DYING to meet you.
8:49 PM 24th Oct 1415 from TavernWiFi

YungFa @ChienFu I bloody would have done.
6.20 PM 12th Jan 1452 from LiaodongOnLine

ChienFu @YungFa I said SOD the Temple in Gansu, when
the Mongols come strolling through here they'll smash it
along with every other bloody thing.
6:21 PM 12th Jan 1452 from MingNet

YungFa @ChienFu Nice one
6:22 PM 12th Jan 1452 from LiaodongOnLine

ChienFu @YungFa He's all "Keep your ponytail on", I said
you'll be lucky to keep your HEAD on if the Emperor sees this.
6:24 PM 12th Jan 1452 from MingNet

YungFa @ChienFu Bet that shut him up.
6:25 PM 12th Jan 1452 from LiaodongOnLine

ChienFu @YungFa Did a bit. Not that the Emperor gives
a monkeys. Sat at home stroking his vases. Him and
his bloody vases.
6:26 PM 12th Jan 1452 from MingNet

YungFa @ChienFu What is it about him and vases? It was
only the thought of Mongols breaking his vases made him
order the wall in the first place.
6:28 PM 12th Jan 1452 from LiaodongOnLine

ChienFu @YungFa Well that got them moving anyway.
It will be impressive when it's finished.
6:29 PM 12th Jan 1452 from MingNet

YungFa @ChienFu Hm, Apparently when it's done you'll
be able to see space from it.
6:31 PM 12th Jan 1452 from LiaodongOnLine

#WAROFTHEROSES

kingrichard3 A horse, a horse my kingdom for a horse!
Will any noble man this day but help find me a horse?
2:18 PM 22nd Aug 1485 from yorknet

HenryTudor @kingrichard3   http://en.wikipedia.org/horse
2:19 PM 22nd Aug 1485 from lancasterweb

kingrichard3 @HenryTudor You're not funny.
2.20 PM 22nd Aug 1485 from yorknet

#MONALISA

LEONARDOdaV @SrDelGiocondo Well it's finished but I don't know what you're gonna think about it.
12:30 PM 15th Jun 1505 from MediciNet

LEONARDOdaV @SrDelGiocondo I mean it looks like Lisa and everything, but there's something... Oh I dunno.
12:31 PM 15th Jun 1505 from MediciNet

LEONARDOdaV @SrDelGiocondo She spent the whole time trying not to giggle. I kept having to check my flies were done up.
12:32 PM 15th Jun 1505 from MediciNet

LEONARDOdaV @SrDelGiocondo I'm trying to paint and she's all like pfff... I'm like WHAT? And she's all Oh nothing, just keep painting, pff. Put me off.
12:33 PM 15th Jun 1505 from MediciNet

LEONARDOdaV @SrDelGiocondo Some sort of private ladies' joke I've no doubt. Can't decide if she's come out looking enigmatic or just a bit smug.
12:34 PM 15th Jun 1505 from MediciNet

LEONARDOdaV @SrDelGiocondo And whose idea was it to shave her eyebrows? I'll paint 'em back in if you like. Might be hip right now but it looks weird.
12:35 PM 15th Jun 1505 from MediciNet

LEONARDOdaV @SrDelGiocondo And she turns up in the drabbest little green number I've ever seen with her hair all unwashed and centre parted.
12:36 PM 15th Jun 1505 from MediciNet

LEONARDOdaV @SrDelGiocondo I was like Lisa, love, you're having your picture done, it's not an act of bloody contrition. Have you got anything a bit sparkly?   :
12:37 PM 15th Jun 1505 from MediciNet

LEONARDOdaV @SrDelGiocondo And she said Just get your easel out, Da Whatever Your Name Is, our Francesco's paying for this.
12:38 PM 15th Jun 1505 from MediciNet

LEONARDOdaV @SrDelGiocondo Then she said "and don't do us with four arms like you did that bloke" I said IT'S NOT A BLOKE WITH FOUR – oh never mind.
12:39 PM 15th Jun 1505 from MediciNet

LEONARDOdaV @SrDelGiocondo Which reminds me, I'll send young Giacomo round with the invoice on Monday. Fees as arranged. I'll do you 10% off for cash.
12:40 PM 15th Jun 1505 from MediciNet

#AZTECS

Tlaxalacl @Iztazuma See the sacrifice yesterday?
9:13 AM 2nd Mar 1521 from MontezumaNet

Iztazuma @Tlaxalacl Couldn't mate, bringing the beans in.
Good one?
9:14 AM 2nd Mar 1521 from TexcocoOnLine

Tlaxalacl @Iztazuma Not really. You missed nothing. Which is more
than can be said for Hetzcoatl.
9:15 AM 2nd Mar 1521 from MontezumaNet

Iztazuma @Tlaxalacl It wasn't Hetzcoatl on the knife again?!
FFS he's useless.
9:16 AM 2nd Mar 1521 from TexcocoOnLine

Tlaxalacl @Iztazuma I know, why they keep sending him out I can't
imagine. Doesn't know one end of a knife from the other.
9.17 AM 2nd Mar 1521 from MontezumaNet

Iztazuma @Tlaxalacl He's keen, I'll give him that. What he lacks in
precision he makes up for in enthusiasm.
9:18 AM 2nd Mar 1521 from TexcocoOnLine

Tlaxalacl @Iztazuma You're not kidding They're still trying to get
the temple steps clean. He'll never make High Priest unless he
sorts his aim out.
9:19 AM 2nd Mar 1521 from MontezumaNet

Iztazuma @Tlaxalacl He's not ready for the big leagues, certainly. How many thrusts this time?
9:21 AM 2nd Mar 1521 from TexcocoOnLine

Tlaxalacl @Iztazuma I stopped counting after seven. It was the poor sod on the altar I felt sorry for, he didn't know where to look.
9:22 AM 2nd Mar 1521 from MontezumaNet

Iztazuma @Tlaxalacl You've got to feel for the lad, all keyed up for the big day and then the moment's ruined by a display of rank amateurism.
9:23 AM 2nd Mar 1521 from TexcocoOnLine

Tlaxalacl @Iztazuma Well at least he missed the worst bit.
9:24 AM 2nd Mar 1521 from MontezumaNet

Iztazuma @Tlaxalacl Oh yes? Do tell.
9:25 AM 2nd Mar 1521 from TexcocoOnLine

Tlaxalacl @Iztazuma Lad finally stops wiggling, Hetz reaches for the heart, holds it aloft in veneration to Huitzilopochtli, we all piss ourselves.
9:27 AM 2nd Mar 1521 from MontezumaNet

Iztazuma @Tlaxalacl Oh no don't tell me.
9:28 AM 2nd Mar 1521 from TexcocoOnLine

Tlaxalacl @Iztazuma He's only got his bloody pancreas, hasn't he.
9:29 AM 2nd Mar 1521 from MontezumaNet

Iztazuma @Tlaxalacl Oh dear oh dear.
9:30 AM 2nd Mar 1521 from TexcocoOnLine

Tlaxalacl @Iztazuma We're all giving it "You're not appeasing anybody with that, son", he shoves it back in and acts like we haven't noticed.
9:31 AM 2nd Mar 1521 from MontezumaNet

Iztazuma @Tlaxalacl He'll be lucky to be picked again this year.
9:32 AM 2nd Mar 1521 from TexcocoOnLine

Tlaxalacl @Iztazuma Well he might get another go, but not on THAT end of the knife, if you know what I mean.
9:33 AM 2nd Mar 1521 from MontezumaNet

Iztazuma @Tlaxalacl Steady. Gotta go, I've left Tocloc in charge of the stall.
9:34 AM 2nd Mar 1521 from TexcocoOnLine

Tlaxalacl @Iztazuma Blimey. On you go son, ta-da.
9:35 AM 2nd Mar 1521 from MontezumaNet

#THEREFORMATION

MartyLuther Crumbs, it's all gone off a bit since I nailed that letter to the church door. #95theses
6:20 PM 3rd Jan 1521 from Wittenberry

MartyLuther Apparently the bishops are concocting some sort of punishment for me. #95theses
6:23 PM 3rd Jan 1521 from Wittenberry

MartyLuther Ew! Ew! Just heard what the bishops want me to do and it's DISGUSTING. #95theses
12:04 PM 5th Jan 1521 from Wittenberry

MartyLuther Apart from anything else it's unenforceable. What are they going to do, watch me 24 hours a day and make sure that's all I eat? #95theses
12:07 PM 5th Jan 1521 from Wittenberry

MartyLuther Oh, ok. Turns out "Diet Of Worms" is just the name of the tribunal. In the town of Worms. Phew! #95theses
10:17 AM 6th Jan 1521 from Wittenberry

MartyLuther @DietOfWorms Here I stand. I can do no other.
9:12 AM 15th Jan 1521 from Wittenberry

MartyLuther @DietOfWorms No really, someone's standing on the hem of me cassock, I can't move.
9:14 AM 15th Jan 1521 from Wittenberry

#THESIXWIVESOF HENRYVIII

catherineparr So girls, what's he like?
4:13 PM 11th Jul 1543 from consortweb

anneofcleves @catherineparr He's an idiot. Good luck – you'll need it.
4:14 PM 11th Jul 1543 from consortweb

catherineparr @anneofcleves Really? Oh God. Was hoping it wouldn't be that bad.
4:15 PM 11th Jul 1543 from consortweb

anneofcleves RT @catherineparr Was hoping it wouldn't be that bad (!!!)
4:15 PM 11th Jul 1543 from consortweb

catherinehoward @anneofcleves is right. Plus he stinks.
4:17 PM 11th Jul 1543 from dissolutionnet

catherineofaragon hello everyone. Let me just add that he gave me syphilis.
4:18 PM 11th Jul 1543 from infantatweet

catherinehoward He threatened to cut my head off!
4:19 PM 11th Jul 1543 from dissolutionnet

catherineparr @catherinehoward NFW!
4:19 PM 11th Jul 1543 from consortweb

catherinehoward @catherineparr Way! In fact I'm expecting
it any day now.
4:20 PM 11th Jul 1543 from dissolutionnet

anneofcleves He had our marriage annulled.
4:22 PM 11th Jul 1543 from consortweb

catherineofaragon @anneofcleves Thought you were divorced?
4:23 PM 11th Jul 1543 from infantatweet

anneofcleves @catherineofaragon Common misconception.
4:24 PM 11th Jul 1543 from consortweb

catherineparr Hang on hang on back up everyone – I think I need
to know more about these heads being cut off!
4:24 PM 11th Jul 1543 from consortweb

catherinehoward @catherineparr Basically if you don't give him a
male heir he doesn't half bear a grudge.
4:25 PM 11th Jul 1543 from dissolutionnet

anneofcleves @catherineparr honestly he can be a right sod.
4:26 PM 11th Jul 1543 from consortweb

catherineparr Oh GREAT! :-(
4:26 PM 11th Jul 1543 from consortweb

anneofcleves @catherineparr He's a bloke. He thinks simply
chopping a head off will help solve everything.
4:27 PM 11th Jul 1543 from consortweb

catherineofaragon just DM @anneboleyn and ask her.
Oh wait – you can't!
4:29 PM 11th Jul 1543 from infantatweet

anneofcleves @catherineofaragon LOL
4:29 PM 11th Jul 1543 from consortweb

catherineparr is Jane Seymour on twitter? Just done
a search but I can't find her.
4:34 PM 11th Jul 1543 from consortweb

anneofcleves she was – but she's not any more.
4:35 PM 11th Jul 1543 from consortweb

catherinehoward she died in childbirth.
4:35 PM 11th Jul 1543 from dissolutionnet

catherineparr Oh for heaven's sake.
4:35 PM 11th Jul 1543 from consortweb

#THECOLONISATION OFAMERICA

MylesS Not the smoothest of landings, but still, we're here. #colony
1:12 PM 11th Nov 1620 from MayflowerFreeWiFi

MylesS We had the whole coast of an unspoiled continent to aim at, and we landed on a ROCK. Nice going. #colony
1:15 PM 11th Nov 1620 from MayflowerFreeWiFi

ChrisMartinnotthatone This place is bleak, wet, cold and filled with unknown terrors and hazards. Let's call it Plymouth. #colony
1:24 PM 11th Nov 1620 from PuritanPhone

WmBrewster At last! In this new and unsullied land we shall be delivered from the religious oppression of the English crown! #colony
2:03 PM 11th Nov 1620 from PilgrimNet

SteveH Halleluiah! #colony
2:04 PM 11th Nov 1620 from PuritanMobile

WmBrewster And we will be free to get on with the sacred task of oppressing OURSELVES! #colony
2:05 PM 11th Nov 1620 from PilgrimNet

SteveH Hooray! #colony
2:06 PM 11th Nov 1620 from SettlerPhone

WmBrewster Is someone cheering? #colony
2:07 PM 11th Nov 1620 from PilgrimNet

SteveH Sorry. #colony
2:08 PM 11th Nov 1620 from SettlerPhone

WmBrewster Bloody well think so. #colony
2:09 PM 11th Nov 1620 from PilgrimNet

SteveH I say, I've just met some rather dusky chaps with
no shirts and arseless leather trousers. #colony
10:24 PM 11th Nov 1620 from SettlerPhone

WmBrewster Good lord. I've never seen someone so in
need of a bit of oppression in my life. #colony
10:33 PM 11th Nov 1620 from PilgrimNet

WmBrewster Let's get to it then! I think I'm going to
like it here. #colony
10:40 PM 11th Nov 1620 from PilgrimNet

#THEGUNPOWDER PLOT

g_fawkes The first rule of Gunpowder Club: YOU DO NOT TALK ABOUT GUNPOWDER CLUB #gunpowdertreason&plot
9:15 AM 12th Mar 1605 from BombBerry

BobCatesby @g_fawkes Actually that's the second rule. The FIRST rule is NO SMOKING #gunpowdertreason&plot
9:17 AM 12th Mar 1605 from DeiPhone

#THEGREAT FIREOFLONDON

puddinglanebaker just popped out.
11:58 PM 2nd Sep 1666 from jammydoughNet

puddinglanebaker Hope I didn't leave the oven on.
11:59 PM 2nd Sep 1666 from jammydoughNet

#PIRATES

longjohnsilver @billybones Retweet this #blackspot to @BlindPew
3:21 PM 3rd Oct 1650 from parrottweet

billybones @BlindPew RT @longjohnsilver #blackspot
3:22 PM 3rd Oct 1650 from galleonNet

BlindPew RT @billybones @longjohnsilver #blackspot
3:23 PM 3rd Oct 1650 from patchNet

captainkidd RT @BlindPew @billybones @longjohnsilver
#blackspot
3:24 PM 3rd Oct 1650 from xmarksthetweet

CpnBlackBeard RT @Captainkidd @BlindPew @billybones
@longjohnsilver #blackspot
3:25 PM 3rd Oct 1650 from MrPlank

Bluebeard RT @Blackbeard @Captainkidd @BlindPew @billybones
@longjohnsilver #blackspot
3:26 PM 3rd Oct 1650 from poopdeck

BlackSam RT @Bluebeard @Blackbeard @Captainkidd @BlindPew @
billybones @longjohnsilver #blackspot
3:27 PM 3rd Oct 1650 from yohohomobile

Captainflint RT @BlackSam @Bluebeard @Blackbeard @Captainkidd
@BlindPew @billybones @longjohnsilver #blackspot
3:28 PM 3rd Oct 1650 from skullandcrosstwit

BennGunn RT @Captainflint @BlackSam @Bluebeard @Blackbeard @Captainkidd @BlindPew @billybones @longjohnsilver #blackspot
3:29 PM 3rd Oct 1650 from TreasureWeb

jimhawkins RT @BennGunn @Captainflint @BlackSam @Bluebeard @Blackbeard @Captainkidd @BlindPew @billybones @longjohnsilver #blackspot
3:30 PM 3rd Oct 1650 from yohO2

MaryRead Boys boys boys boys boys. For heaven's sake, grow up.
3:32 PM 3rd Oct 1650 from twitterwench

#THEGREAT
COMPOSERS

WolfgangAM Ach, guys, I have completely forgotten that the Emperor's birthday next week is being.
12:15 PM 9th Mar 1788 from ViennaWeb

JoeHaydn @WolfgangAM Uh-oh. :O What you are going to do?
12:16 PM 9th Mar 1788 from AustriaOnLine

WolfgangAM There is totally not enough time for a whole opera together getting. I will have to something simple outknock. Ideas anybody?
12:17 PM 9th Mar 1788 from ViennaWeb

LudVanB @WolfgangAM LOUD. Something LOUD be writing. You must the cobwebs from the old geezer's ears blow!
12:19 PM 9th Mar 1788 from BonnBerry

WolfgangAM @LudVanB Ach, young Ludwig, always with the everything-really-loud-all-the-time-must-be. It will no good do you.
12:21 PM 9th Mar 1788 from ViennaWeb

WolfgangAM Come on, composerfriends! Out here me help!
12:25 PM 9th Mar 1788 from ViennaWeb

ASalieri01 @WolfgangAM Well, if you are really stuck, I – but no. You would never be interested in any of my thoughts.
12:28 PM 9th Mar 1788 from KapellmeisterNet

WolfgangAM @ASalieri01 Hey Tony, I am here the
creek up with no paddles having. What you got?
12:29 PM 9th Mar 1788 from ViennaWeb

ASalieri01 @WolfgangAM Is just a trifle, a mere fancy,
is not even really a tune, is just an idea.
12:31 PM 9th Mar 1788 from KapellmeisterNet

WolfgangAM @ASalieri01 Tease me not Tony! On me it be laying!
12:32 PM 9th Mar 1788 from ViennaWeb

ASalieri01 @WolfgangAM Well I have a simple melody
– you will no doubt improve it beyond measure – and a title.
12:34 PM 9th Mar 1788 from KapellmeisterNet

WolfgangAM @ASalieri01 Is good! Is good! What is the title?
12:36 PM 9th Mar 1788 from ViennaWeb

ASalieri01 @WolfgangAM In honour of his Imperial Majesty
I have called the piece "L'Imperatore è un Grande Ano"
12:38 PM 9th Mar 1788 from KapellmeisterNet

WolfgangAM @ASalieri01 Sounds cool! What means it?
12:39 PM 9th Mar 1788 from ViennaWeb

ASalieri01 @WolfgangAM Is a mean "Have a great year, Emperor"
12:41 PM 9th Mar 1788 from KapellmeisterNet

WolfgangAM @ASalieri01 Fantastic! I am so glad a friend
like you to have, Tony.
12:42 PM 9th Mar 1788 from ViennaWeb

ASalieri01 @WolfgangAM Don't mention it. No really, don't.
12:43 PM 9th Mar 1788 from KapellmeisterNet

#BATTLEOF TRAFALGAR

MisterHardy Arse, just as I was about to have a drink with the lads to celebrate kicking the French, the Admiral wants me on deck.
4:09 PM 21st Oct 1805 from VictoryWeb

MisterHardy God, he's not looking well. Always hard to tell with Nelson but still. Better see what he wants. L8rs.
4:11 PM 21st Oct 1805 from VictoryWeb

MisterHardy O-kay, THAT sucked on pretty much every level.
4:20 PM 21st Oct 1805 from VictoryWeb

MisterHardy I mean, yes he's an Admiral and national hero & everything, but I'm fairly sure that counted as sexual harassment in the workplace.
4:21 PM 21st Oct 1805 from VictoryWeb

MisterHardy I KNEW I only got this gig cos he fancied me. It's like my first commission all over again.
4:24 PM 21st Oct 1805 from VictoryWeb

MisterHardy and I REALLY could have lived without the whole coughing-up-blood thing.
4:23 PM 21st Oct 1805 from VictoryWeb

MisterHardy Surprisingly smooth though. Reminded me of my days in the academy.
4:25 PM 21st Oct 1805 from VictoryWeb

MisterHardy Oh FFS, ship's surgeon says he's karked it. I'm going to be blamed for this, aren't I?
4:30 PM 21st Oct 1805 from VictoryWeb

MisterHardy "Old dog breath Hardy, finished off the Admiral"
That sort of thing ends careers, you know.
4:31 PM 21st Oct 1805 from VictoryWeb

MisterHardy @ArthurWilliamDevis OH NOES don't tell me you were painting that. I'll buy the sketches off you. Please!
4:33 PM 21st Oct 1805 from VictoryWeb

#THEBATTLEOF WATERLOO

DukeOfW My my! At #waterloo Napoleon did surrender!
10:11 PM 18th Jun 1815 from WellyWeb

EarlOfUxbridge Really? Nice going, Arthur. #waterloo
10:13 PM 18th Jun 1815 from PagetNet

generalhalkett #waterloo FTW! Did you give him the boot, Wellington?
10:14 PM 18th Jun 1815 from InfantryMobile

DukeOfW Oh ha bloody ha. #waterloo
10:16 PM 18th Jun 1815 from WellyWeb

generalhalkett Oh lighten up Arthur. #waterloo
10:17 PM 18th Jun 1815 from InfantryMobile

EarlOfUxbridge #waterloo Yeah, what's your beef, Wellington?
10:19 PM 18th Jun 1815 from PagetNet

DukeOfW #waterloo I hate you guys.
10:21 PM 18th Jun 1815 from WellyWeb

 **#THEMADNESSOF KINGGEORGE**

KingGeorge Good morning everyone.
8:04 AM 12th Jan 1818 from royaltwit

KingGeorge I've just pissed in the kettle again.
8:04 AM 12th Jan 1818 from royaltwit

KingGeorge LOL.
8:05 AM 12th Jan 1818 from royaltwit

#THESTOCKTONTO DARLINGTONRAILWAY

georgestephenson Big day today. Opening of the Stockton to Darlington railway. World's first permanent steam locomotive hauled public railway. Yay.
8:47 AM 27th Sep 1825 from rocketweb

georgestephenson it's taken me years to develop these mechanized engines.
8:48 AM 27th Sep 1825 from rocketweb

georgestephenson The trick is to have high-pressure steam from a centre-flue boiler to drive two vertical cylinders.
8:49 AM 27th Sep 1825 from rocketweb

georgestephenson Press are saying it could revolutionize travel.
8:51 AM 27th Sep 1825 from rocketweb

georgestephenson People will be transported around the country in comfort and style.
8:53 AM 27th Sep 1825 from rocketweb

nationalrailenquiries We are sending you this message because you have requested real time journey updates from national rail.
8.54 AM 27th Sep 1825 from web

nationalrailenquiries We would like to apologise for the delay to your service this morning.
8:55 AM 27th Sep 1825 from web

nationalrailenquiries The Stockton to Darlington railway is suspended due to essential engineering works.
8:56 AM 27th Sep 1825 from web

nationalrailenquiries There is a replacement bus service in operation this morning between Stockton and Darlington.
8:57 AM 27th Sep 1825 from web

nationalrailenquiries Or at least there will be, just as soon as someone invents a bus.
8:58 AM 27th Sep 1825 from web

nationalrailenquiries Thank you for subscribing to @nationalrail updates on twitter.
8:59 AM 27th Sep 1825 from web

georgestephenson FFS.
9:00 AM 27th Sep 1825 from rocketweb

#ONTHEORIGIN OFSPECIES

JohnMurray52 @Cdarwin Charlie – just finished the manuscript. It's brilliant! Funniest thing I've ever read! PMSL!
9:31 AM 22nd Jul 1859 from PublisherWeb

JohnMurray52 @Cdarwin The way Lyell was talking it up I thought it was gonna be some dry slog about turtles but this is hysterical. We're gonna OWN xmas.
9:33 AM 22nd Jul 1859 from PublisherWeb

JohnMurray52 @Cdarwin I mean it sags a bit in the middle (the fossils stuff) but I'm sure we can tidy that up. REALLY stoked about this.
9:34 AM 22nd Jul 1859 from PublisherWeb

JohnMurray52 @Cdarwin And that cliff hanger/punchline about the apes and people! You cheeky sod! Let's have lunch, talk about cover shots.
9:35 AM 22nd Jul 1859 from PublisherWeb

JohnMurray52 @Cdarwin Just spoke to Huxley. He says the book isn't supposed to be funny. WTF? Very confused now. Call me asap.
11:15 AM 22nd Jul 1859 from PublisherWeb

JohnMurray52 @Cdarwin But honestly, the idea that everything's related to EVERYTHING ELSE if you go back far enough – do you realise what that means?
11:17 AM 22nd Jul 1859 from PublisherWeb

JohnMurray52 @Cdarwin It means we're ALL related!
I'm related to my wife! Eew! Might as well all be Cornish!
11:18 AM 22nd Jul 1859 from PublisherWeb

JohnMurray52 @Cdarwin and all those gentlemen's
clubs poring through family trees to keep out anyone
remotely Jewish – they'll have to kick EVERYONE out.
11:20 AM 22nd Jul 1859 from PublisherWeb

JohnMurray52 @Cdarwin Obviously the vicars will go
ballistic but sod that, there are more important things
at stake here – think about Christmas.
11:22 AM 22nd Jul 1859 from PublisherWeb

JohnMurray52 @Cdarwin If you're related to every
other living thing on the planet don't you have to invite
them ALL to Christmas dinner? It's insane.
11.23 AM 22nd Jul 1859 from PublisherWeb

JohnMurray52 @Cdarwin Although hang on a minute
– ballistic vicars – let me think about this. L8r.
11:25 AM 22nd Jul 1859 from PublisherWeb

JohnMurray52 @Cdarwin Charlie I've thought it over
and anything which send vicars ballistic is ALWAYS good for
sales. I'm still in. Lunch Monday ok?
1:45 PM 22nd Jul 1859 from PublisherWeb

#THEGETTYSBURG TWEET

ABE1 Four score and seven years ago our fathers brought forth on this continent a new nation, conceived in Liberty, and dedicated to the proposit
10:05 AM 19th Nov 1863 from PrezWeb

ABE1 4 score & 7 years ago our fathers brought forth on this continent a new nation, conceived in Liberty, and dedicated to the proposition that
10:07 AM 19th Nov 1863 from PrezWeb

ABE1 87 years ago our fathers brought forth on this continent a new nation, conceived in Liberty, and dedicated to the proposition that all men a
10:09 AM 19th Nov 1863 from PrezWeb

ABE1 87yr ago R frs brought 4th on this continent a new nation, conceived in Liberty, & dedicated to the prop that all men R created equal(YES!)
10:13 AM 19th Nov 1863 from PrezWeb

ABE1 Now we are engaged in a great civil war, testing whether that nation, or any nation, so conceived and so dedicated, can long endure. We are
10:14 AM 19th Nov 1863 from PrezWeb

ABE1 Now we R in great civ war, testing if that nat, or any nat, so conc'd and so ded'd, can endure. We R met on a great battle-field of that war.
10:17 AM 19th Nov 1863 from PrezWeb

ABE1 We have come to dedicate a portion of that field,
as a final resting place for those who here gave their lives
that that nation might live.
10:18 AM 19th Nov 1863 from PrezWeb

ABE1 (that bit worked quite well) It is altogether
fitting and proper that we should do this. (might just
get this to work after all)
10:20 AM 19th Nov 1863 from PrezWeb

ABE1 But, in a larger sense, we can not dedicate...
we can not consecrate...we can not hallow this ground.
The brave men, living and dead, who str
10:21 AM 19th Nov 1863 from PrezWeb

ABE1 I'm just getting annoyed now.
10:23 AM 19th Nov 1863 from PrezWeb

ABE1 Hang on, I've got an idea.
10:27 AM 19th Nov 1863 from PrezWeb

ABE1 87y ago-NEW nat,prop:all men=.WAR-uh oh.Dedicate field.
GOOD.BUT whatwe say<whatwe do now ie.make sure Gov of
by&4peeps not perish fr Earth.
10:41 AM 19th Nov 1863 from PrezWeb

ABE1 Nailed it. Who wants a drink?
10:42 AM 19th Nov 1863 from PrezWeb

#ALEXANDER GRAHAMBELL

alexandergrahambell @thomaswatson Mr Watson, are you there?
10:00 AM 10th Mar 1876 from electrictwittergraph

thomaswatson @alexandergrahambell Yes.
10:01 AM 10th Mar 1879 from electrictwittergraph

alexandergrahambell @thomaswatson In the adjoining room?
Out of both sight and earshot?
10:02 AM 10th Mar 1876 from electrictwittergraph

thomaswatson @alexandergrahambell Yes.
10.03 AM 10th Mar 1876 from electrictwittergraph

alexandergrahambell @thomaswatson are you ready for the
experiment to commence?
10:04 AM 10th Mar 1876 from electrictwittergraph

thomaswatson @alexandergrahambell Yes.
10:05 AM 10th Mar 1876 from electrictwittergraph

alexandergrahambell @thomaswatson ok here we go then...
10:06 AM 10th Mar 1876 from electrictwittergraph

thomaswatson @alexandergrahambell K.
10:07 AM 10th Mar 1876 from electrictwittergraph

alexandergrahambell @thomaswatson ready?
10:08 AM 10th Mar 1876 from electrictwittergraph

thomaswatson @alexandergrahambell ready.
10:09 AM 10th Mar 1876 from electrictwittergraph

alexandergrahambell @thomaswatson Ok.. 3–2–1...
10:10 AM 10th Mar 1876 from electrictwittergraph

alexandergrahambell @thomaswatson Mr Watson... come here...
I want to see you.
10:11 AM 10th Mar 1876 from electrictwittergraph

alexandergrahambell @thomaswatson There. Could you
read my tweet?
10:12 AM 10th Mar 1876 from electrictwittergraph

thomaswatson @alexandergrahambell yes.
10:13 AM 10th Mar 1876 from electrictwittergraph

alexandergrahambell @thomaswatson Then it is a success.
I have invented Twitter. I must alert the patent office.
10:14 AM 10th Mar 1876 from electrictwittergraph

alexandergrahambell @thomaswatson Actually, Mr Watson,
I can't find my mobile. Can you call it?
10:17 AM 10th Mar 1876 from electrictwittergraph

SigmundFreud Concerned about patient Gustave E. He's shown me plans for this thing he's building in Paris. Worst case of overcompensation I've ever seen.
3:22 PM 19th Oct 1885 from idPhone

SigmundFreud Gustave E's therapy going nowhere. Every time I mention his tower he grabs his crotch and calls me a jealous Austrian pipsqueak.
12:19 PM 26th Oct 1885 from idPhone

SigmundFreud Pleased to report Gustave E finally making progress. Has agreed to revise plans for his tower.
2:28 PM 12th Nov 1885 from idPhone

SigmundFreud Gustave E showed me his new plans; he's cancelled the two enormous domed pergolas he was planning to put either side of the tower.
12:15 PM 15th Nov 1885 from idPhone

SigmundFreud It's still got a big bell-end though.
12:17 PM 15th Nov 1885 from idPhone

#JACKTHERIPPER

jacktheripper @boss, Central News Agency, London. I keep on hearing the police have caught me.
3:25 PM 25th Sep 1888 from slashweb

jacktheripper @boss I am down on whores and I shan't quit ripping them till I do get buckled.
3:25 PM 25th Sep 1888 from slashweb

jacktheripper @boss I saved some of the proper red stuff in a ginger beer bottle over the last job to write with but it went thick like glue and I cant use it.
3:26 PM 25th Sep 1888 from slashweb

jacktheripper @boss So I'm tweeting instead ha ha.
3:27 PM 25th Sep 1888 from slashweb

jacktheripper @boss My knife's so nice and sharp I want to get to work right away.
3:28 PM 25th Sep 1888 from slashweb

jacktheripper @boss You will never catch me. My identity is beyond your grasp. Yours truly, @jacktheripper
3.29 PM 25th Sep 1888 from slashweb

DetInspFrederickAbberline @jacktheripper You do realise we can just trace your ip address?
3:32 PM 25th Sep 1888 from TweetNick

jacktheripper @DetInspFrederickAbberline Really? Shit.
3:33 PM 25th Sep 1888 from slashweb

#PAVLOV'SDOG

pavlov Rang bell. Dog ate food.
5:00 PM 9th Dec 1901 from приятеля родословнойtwit

pavlov Rang bell. Dog ate food.
5:00 PM 10th Dec 1901 from приятеля родословнойtwit

pavlov Rang bell. Dog ate food.
5:00 PM 11th Dec 1901 from приятеля родословнойtwit

pavlov Rang bell. Dog ate food.
5:00 PM 12th Dec 1901 from приятеля родословнойtwit

pavlov Rang bell. Dog ate food.
5:00 PM 13th Dec 1901 from приятеля родословнойtwit

pavlov Rang bell. Dog ate food.
5:00 PM 14th Dec 1901 from приятеля родословнойtwit

pavlov Rang bell. Dog ate food.
5:00 PM 15th Dec 1901 from приятеля родословнойtwit

pavlov Rang bell. Dog ate food.
5:00 PM 16th Dec 1901 from приятеля родословнойtwit

pavlov Rang bell. Dog ate food.
5:00 PM 17th Dec 1901 from приятеля родословнойtwit

pavlov Rang bell. Dog ate food.
5:00 PM 18th Dec 1901 from приятеля родословнойtwit

pavlov Rang bell. Dog ate food.
5:00 PM 19th Dec 1901 from приятеля родословнойtwit

pavlov Rang bell. Dog ate food.
5:00 PM 20th Dec 1901 from приятеля родословнойtwit

pavlov Rang bell. Dog ate food.
5:00 PM 22nd Dec 1901 from приятеля родословнойtwit

pavlov Rang bell. Dog ate food.
5:00 PM 23rd Dec 1901 from приятеля родословнойtwit

pavlov Rang bell. Dog ate food.
5:00 PM 24th Dec 1901 from приятеля родословнойtwit

pavlov Rang bell. Dog ate food. Happy Christmas everyone.
5:00 PM 25th Dec 1901 from приятеля родословнойtwit

pavlov Rang bell. Dog ate food.
5:00 PM 26th Dec 1901 from приятеля родословнойtwit

pavlov Rang bell. Dog ate food.
5:00 PM 27th Dec 1901 from приятеля родословнойtwit

pavlov Rang bell. Dog ate food.
5:00 PM 28th Dec 1901 from приятеля родословнойtwit

pavlov Rang bell. Dog ate food.
5:00 PM 29th Dec 1901 from приятеля родословнойtwit

pavlov Rang bell. Dog ate food.
5:00 PM 30th Dec 1901 приятеля родословнойtwit

pavlov Rang bell. Dog *didn't* eat food.
5:00 PM 31st Dec 1901 from приятеля родословнойtwit

pavlov Tits. Back to the drawing board.
5:01 PM 31st Dec 1901 from приятеля родословнойtwit

#SCOTTOFTHE ANTARCTIC

captainoates More adverse weather today.
Whole expedition weakening.
6:04 AM 16th Mar 1912 from snowmobile

captainoates My calculations indicate that we need maintain a
march of over 9 miles a day in order to have full rations.
6:05 AM 16th Mar 1912 from snowmobile

captainoates I fear the worst. The ponies lack the strength to
pull the sled.
6:07 AM 16th Mar 1912 from snowmobile

captainoates @scottoftheantarctic's ignorance about marching
with animals is colossal.
6:08 AM 16th Mar 1912 from snowmobile

captainoates Myself, I dislike @scottoftheantarctic intensely and
would chuck the whole thing if it were not that we are a British
expedition.
6:09 AM 16th Mar 1912 from snowmobile

captainoates Plus it's bloody freezing in this tent and
@scottoftheantarctic is hogging the all the fur again.
6:10 AM 16th Mar 1912 from snowmobile

captainoates And he ate the last bit of Kendal mint cake.
6:10 AM 16th Mar 1912 from snowmobile

captainoates And did he help to put the tent up last night?
Did he f**k.
6:11 AM 16th Mar 1912 from snowmobile

captainoates Jesus it's cold. Fingers getting too numb too tweet.
6:14 AM 16th Mar 1912 from snowmobile

captainoates Oh ffs @scottoftheantarctric just farted.
6:20 AM 16th Mar 1912 from snowmobile

captainoates he farted in a tiny tent the dirty bastard.
6:20 AM 16th Mar 1912 from snowmobile

captainoates I'm simply not sure how much longer I can go on.
6:21 AM 16th Mar 1912 from snowmobile

captainoates @scottoftheantarctic has just farted again.
6:22 AM 16th Mar 1912 from snowmobile

captainoates I'm going to log out now. I may be some time.
6:25 AM 16th Mar 1912 from snowmobile

#THESINKINGOF THETITANIC

deckhand Arranging deckchairs.
7:33 AM 12th Apr 1912 from tweetondeck

deckhand Again.
7:36 AM 12th Apr 1912 from tweetondeck

deckhand That's all I do all day – arrange the deckchairs.
Wish I'd never taken this job.
7:42 AM 12th Apr 1912 from tweetondeck

deckhand Still arranging deckchairs.
4.:4 PM 12th Apr 1912 from tweetondeck

deckhand Another day, another dollar of arranging deckchairs.
7:31 AM 13th Apr 1912 from tweetondeck

deckhand Lunch.
1:00 PM 13th Apr 1912 from tweetondeck

deckhand Arranging deckchairs.
3:52 PM 13th Apr 1912 from tweetondeck

deckhand Guess what?
7:36 AM 14th Apr 1912 from tweetondeck

deckhand Woah! What was that scraping noise?
11:40 PM 14th Apr 1912 from tweetondeck

deckhand Bugger.
11:56 PM 14th Apr 1912 from tweetondeck

deckhand Just been upstairs. My deckchairs are
all over the bloody place.
12:14 AM 15th Apr 1912 from tweetondeck

deckhand Everyone running for their lives.
12:25 AM 15th Apr 1912 from tweetondeck

deckhand Seems we're all going to die.
1:05 AM 15th Apr 1912 from tweetondeck

deckhand Band's still playing.
1:13 AM 15th Apr 1912 from tweetondeck

deckhand Oh well.
1:22 AM 15th Apr 1912 from tweetondeck

deckhand What can you do?
1:23 AM 15th Apr 1912 from tweetondeck

deckhand Arranging deckchairs.
1:24 AM 15th Apr 1912 from tweetondeck

#WARPOETS

rupertbrooke in a corner of a foreign field.
4:43 PM 12th Sep 1917 from trenchtweet

rupertbrooke hope I don't die or anything.
4:44 PM 12th Sep 1917 from trenchtweet

rupertbrooke but if I do, think this of me
4:44 PM 12th Sep 1917 from trenchtweet

rupertbrooke that there shall be in that rich earth a richer dust concealed.
4:45 PM 12th Sep 1917 from trenchtweet

SiegfriedSassoon @rupertbrooke I was actually thinking 'what are you doing in the *corner* of the field? You're an obvious target there. You're boxed in'.
4:47 PM 12th Sep 1917 from PoetDeck

rupertbrooke @SiegfriedSassoon what?
4:48 PM 12th Sep 1917 from trenchtweet

SiegfriedSassoon @rupertbrooke Well you should at least be on the flat edge of the field, thus leaving yourself numerous avenues of escape from any attack.
4:49 PM 12th Sep 1917 from PoetDeck

SiegfriedSassoon @rupertbrooke Are you not familiar with the expression 'backed into a corner'?
4:49 PM 12th Sep 1917 from PoetDeck

rupertbrooke Think of me a dust whom England bore, shaped, made aware gave once her flowers to love.
4:51 PM 12th Sep 1917 from trenchtweet

SiegfriedSassoon @rupertbrooke More like 'I tell you what, that idiot's going to get himself killed.'
4:53 PM 12th Sep 1917 from PoetDeck

SiegfriedSassoon @rupertbrooke That's what I think.
4:54 PM 12th Sep 1917 from PoetDeck

SiegfriedSassoon RT @rupertbrooke in a corner of a foreign field.
5:01 PM 12th Sep 1917 from PoetDeck

SiegfriedSassoon @rupertbrooke hasn't tweeted for a while now.
5:11 PM 12th Sep 1917 from PoetDeck

SiegfriedSassoon You know what, I've been thinking that this war isn't for me.
5:16 PM 12th Sep 1917 from PoetDeck

SiegfriedSassoon Really dangerous. I'm actually thinking of getting out of the war poetry game.
5:16 PM 12th Sep 1917 from PoetDeck

SiegfriedSassoon thinking about going into hairdressing with my brother @vidal1.
5:18 PM 12th Sep 1917 from PoetDeck

wilfredowen dulce est decorum est.
5:20 PM 12th Sep 1917 from wartwit

SiegfriedSassoon RT @wilfredowen dulce est decorum est.
5:21 PM 12th Sep 1917 from PoetDeck

SiegfriedSassoon Jesus. You poncy twat.
5:21 PM 12th Sep 1917 from PoetDeck

wilfredowen @SiegfriedSassoon. Sod off. It's better than your stuff.
I've read 'Does It Matter?'. It was mawkish shit.
5:22 PM 12th Sep 1917 from wartwit

SiegfriedSassoon @wilfredowen just because you know Latin.
doesn't make you better than me you know
5:23 PM 12th Sep 1914 from PoetDeck

wilfredowen @siegfriedsassoon Have you heard from
@rupertbrooke recently? Did he ever get out of that paddock?
5:24 PM 12th Sep 1917 from wartwit

SiegfriedSassoon I reckon he bought the farm.
5:25 PM 12th Sep 1917 from PoetDeck

wilfredowen @SiegfriedSassoon really? Good investment. S'pose
farming would provide an income after the war. Not much money
in this poetry bollocks.
5:26 PM 12th Sep 1917 from wartwit

SiegfriedSassoon no you dick I mean I reckon he got killed.
5:27 PM 12th Sep 1917 from PoetDeck

wilfredowen oh.
5:28 PM September 12 1917 from wartwit

siegfriedsassoon I've got a joke #deadpoetssociety
5:25 PM 12th Sep 1917 from PoetDeck

wilfredowen @SiegfriedSassoon go on then. #deadpoetssociety
5:25 PM 12th Sep 1917 from wartwit

SiegfriedSassoon why would @rupertbrooke make a good
hairdresser? #deadpoetssociety
5:26 PM 12th Sep 1917 from PoetDeck

SiegfriedSassoon I don't know #deadpoetssociety
5:27 PM 12th Sep 1917 from wartwit

SiegfriedSassoon Because they found his head and shoulders in a trench #deadpoetssociety
5:27 PM 12th Sep 1917 from PoetDeck

wilfredowen LOL ROFL.
5:28 PM 12th Sep 1917 from wartwit

rupertbrooke Guys – I'm actually fine, battery was dead.
5:35 PM 12th Sep 1917 from trenchtweet

SiegfriedSassoon Oh.
5:36 PM 12th Sep 1917 from PoetDeck

#THEHINDENBURG
DISASTER

ErnstS It's no good, I can't wait until we land, I'm gasping for a cigarette.
7:24 PM 6th May 1937 from ZeppelinWeb

ErnstS Oh the humanity.
7:25 PM 6th May 1937 from ZeppelinWeb

#WORLDWARII

winstonchurchill Anyone think of anything that rhymes with 'beaches'?
10:09 AM 4th May 1940 from numbertentwit

anthonyeden1 @winstonchurchill why?
10:10 AM 4th May 1940 from cabiNet

winstonchurchill @anthonyeden1 trying to jazz speech up. Thought I might do one in couplets.
10:10 AM 4th May 1940 from numbertentwit

anthonyeden1 @winstonchurchill I wouldn't. People might not take it seriously.
10:11 AM 4th May 1940 from cabiNet

winstonchurchill @anthonyeden1 Trying to be a bit lighter. Not so depressing. Cheer people up a bit. There's a war on.
10:12 AM 4th May 1940 from numbertentwit

anthonyeden1 @winstonchurchill I think you should keep it serious.
10:13 AM 4th May 1940 from cabiNet

winstonchurchill @anthonyeden1 What do you reckon to "we should fight them on the landing grounds / But with cheery smiles instead of frowns"?
10:16 AM 4th May 1940 from numbertentwit

anthonyeden1 @winstonchurchill You're not serious?
10:16 AM 4th May 1940 from cabiNet

winstonchurchill @anthonyeden1 Sure I am. War would be a whole lot less miserable if people brought smiles instead of guns.
10:17 AM 4th May 1940 from numbertentwit

anthonyeden1 @winstonchurchill Are you alright?
10:18 AM 4th May 1940 from cabinet

winstonchurchill @anthonyeden1 It only takes one muscle to smile but 10,000 muscles to shoot someone in the face.
10:19 AM 4th May 1940 from numbertentwit

winstonchurchill @anthonyeden1 What do you reckon?
10:22 AM 4th May 1940 from numbertentwit

anthonyeden1 @winstonchurchill I reckon you're the PM and you have to be forceful and strong in the face of the enemy.
Show leadership.
10:23 AM 4th May 1940 from cabiNet

winstonchurchill @anthonyeden1 I AM showing leadership.
I just think we could all be a bit nicer. Also thinking of changing my image.
10:25 AM 4th May 1940 from numbertentwit

winstonchurchill @anthonyeden1 Might swap bowler hat for deely boppers and cigar for pipe that blows bubbles.
10:25 AM 4th May 1940 from numbertentwit

anthonyeden1 @winstonchurchill Right. I see what's going on here. You're pissed again aren't you?
10:25 AM 4th May 1940 from cabiNet

winstonchurchill @anthonyeden1 Absolutely hammered old boy.
10:26 AM 4th May 1940 from numbertentwit

anthonyeden1 @winstonchurchill Oh good grief. Just sober up and finish the damn speech. You're addressing the nation in an hour.
10:26 AM 4th May 1940 from cabiNet

winstonchurchill @anthonyeden1 whatever.
10:27 PM 4th May 1940 from numbertentwit

hughcornwellfromthestranglers @winstonchurchill try 'peaches'
10:31 AM 4th May 1977 from timetraveltweet

anthonyeden1 @hughcornwellfromthestranglers Sorry. He's not doing stupid rhymes anymore. You can keep your beaches and peaches.
10:32 AM 4th May 1940 from cabiNet

hughcornwellfromthestranglers @anthonyeden1 cheers. Quite pleased with that couplet. Never know when it might come in handy.
10:34 AM 4th May 1977 from timetraveltweet

winstonchurchill *burps*
10:35 AM 4th May 1940 from numbertentwit

 **#NAZIS**

HeinHimmler Lebensraum Baba #nazipuddings
3:32 PM 12th Feb 1941 from ÜberNet

DrJosefG Hermann GöRing Donuts #nazipuddings
3:33 PM 12th Feb 1941 from ichFön

MartyBmann Albert S-pear tart #nazipuddings
3:34 PM 12th Feb 1941 from DeutschlandÜberLine

RudiHeß Führermisu #nazipuddings
3:36 PM 12th Feb 1941 from Brombeere

BigHGöring #nazipuddings I can't think of one. Got a #nazibiscuits
3:39 PM 12th Feb 1941 from LüftWebbe

DrJosefG Go on then #nazipuddings
3:40 PM 12th Feb 1941 from ichFön

BigHGöring Reinhard HeydRich Tea #nazibiscuits
3:41 PM 12th Feb 1941 from LüftWebbe

HeinHimmler @BigHGöring That was rubbish #göringfail
3:42 PM 12th Feb 1941 from ÜberNet

DerRealFuhrer @HeinHimmler @DrJosefG @MartyBmann @RudiHeß
@BigHGöring Are you gentlemen bored or something?
3:43 PM 12th Feb 1941 from TweetBunker

DrJosefG @DerRealFuhrer Sorry mein Führer
3:44 PM 12th Feb 1941 from ichFön

DerRealFuhrer Don't put yourself out, I mean it's not like we're trying to take over the world or anything. #nazipuddings indeed.
3:45 PM 12th Feb 1941 from TweetBunker

BigHGöring @DerRealFührer Yes sorry mein Führer.
3:46 PM 12th Feb 1941 from LüftWebbe

HeinHimmler Sorry Adolf @DrJosefG @MartyBmann @RudiHess @BigHGöring back to work everybody.
3:46 PM 12th Feb 1941 from ÜberNet

DerRealFührer @HeinHimmler @DrJosefG @MartyBmann @RudiHeß @BigHGöring AND....?
3:47 PM 12th Feb 1941 from TweetBunker

HeinHimmler Sorry #heilhitler
3:47 PM 12th Feb 1941 from ÜberNet

DrJosefG #heilhitler
3:47 PM 12th Feb 1941 from ichFön

MartyBmann #heilhitler
3:47 PM 12th Feb 1941 from DeutschlandÜberLine

RudiHeß #heilhitler
3:47 PM 12th Feb 1941 from Brombeere

BigHGöring #heilhitler
3:47 PM 12th Feb 1941 from LüftWebbe

DerRealFührer @HeinHimmler @DrJosefG @MartyBmann @RudiHeß @BigHGöring That's more bloody like it.
3:48 PM 12th Feb 1941 from TweetBunker

DerRealFührer Can't believe nobody did ReichsPudding #nazipuddings
3:54 PM 12th Feb 1941 from TweetBunker

#MORENAZIS

alberthallcleaner F**king hell. You'll never guess what my hoover just picked up.
7:12 AM 30th Apr 1945 from clothnet

#THETWITTER FEEDOFANNEFRANK

annefrank @kitty It is a wonder that I haven't abandoned all my ideals, they seem so absurd and impractical.
9:44 AM 4th Aug 1944 from twitterhuis

annefrank @kitty Yet I cling to them because I still believe, in spite of everything, that people are truly good at heart.
9:45 AM 4th Aug 1944 from twitterhuis

annefrank This annex is an ideal place to hide in.
Out of sight up the stairs concealed behind the secret bookcase on the 3rd floor.
9:46 AM 4th Aug 1944 from twitterhuis

annefrank Uh-oh. That wasn't a Direct Message was it?
9:48 AM 4th Aug 1944 from twitterhuis

annefrank that went to everyone didn't it?
9:48 AM 4th Aug 1944 from twitterhuis

SchutzstaffelOberscharführerKarlSilberbauer @annefrank Ja. Yes.
9:49 AM 4th Aug 1944 from twitterhuis

SchutzstaffelOberscharführerKarlSilberbauer @annefrank
See you in einer minute mein fraulein.
9:49 AM 4th Aug 1944 from twitterhuis

annefrank Oh arse.
9:50 AM 4th Aug 1944 from twitterhuis

 **#THEDAMBUSTERS**

AirViceMarshallRalphAlexanderCochrane
@wingcommanderguygibson Now listen up my good fellow,
only I've been talking to the rest of the chaps ...
9:39 PM 16th May 1943 from twitterbomber

AirViceMarshallRalphAlexanderCochrane
@wingcommanderguygibson .... and we really don't think you can
legitimately get away with calling your dog that.
9:39 PM 16th May 1943 from twitterbomber

wingcommanderguygibson
@AirViceMarshallRalphAlexanderCochrane *sulks*
9:40 PM 16th May 1943 from twitterbomber

#HIROSHIMA

CaptainRobertA.Lewis Quick trip over to Japan today. Six hours flight time. Just heading to plane now.
7:19 AM 6th Aug 1945 from bombdeck

CaptainRobertA.Lewis Holy shit. The Enola what? No way. There is NO WAY I'm flying that.
7:33 AM 6th Aug 1945 from bombdeck

CaptainRobertA.Lewis Honestly, what twat called it that? No way. We'll be a laughing stock.
7:34 AM 6th Aug 1945 from bombdeck

GroupCmmndrColPaulTibbets @CaptainRobertA.Lewis it's named after my mother.
7:36 AM 6th Aug 1945 from flitedeck

CaptainRobertA.Lewis @ GroupCmmndrColPaulTibbets Oops. Sorry. My bad.
7:35 AM 6th Aug1945 from bombdeck

CaptainRobertA.Lewis @ GroupCmmndrColPaulTibbets You've got to admit though, it's a f**king crap name for a plane.
7:36 AM 6th Aug 1945 from bombdeck

CaptainRobertA.Lewis Everyone will just be laughing at this mission for the rest of time.
7:38 AM 6th Aug 1945 from bombdeck

GroupCmmndrColPaulTibbets @ CaptainRobertA.Lewis You wait 'til you see what someone's written on the side of the nuke.
7:40 AM 6th Aug 1945 from flitedeck

CaptainRobertA.Lewis @GroupCmmndrColPaulTibbets Oh f**k. What?
7:40 AM 6th Aug 1945 from bombdeck

GroupCmmndrColPaulTibbets @CaptainRobertA.Lewis "Little Boy."
7:41 AM 6th Aug 1945 from flitedeck

CaptainRobertA.Lewis @GroupCmmndrColPaulTibbets Jesus H Truman. It gets worse. That is sooo lame.
7:42 AM 6th Aug 1945 from bombdeck

HiroDude Nice day. Looking up and it's clear skies all the way!!!11! Not a cloud to be seen. Lovely. Have a feeling today's gonna be a hot one.
8:10 AM 6th Aug 1945 from web

HiroDude Blimey. That planes coming in low.
8:14 AM 6th Aug 1945 from web

HiroDude What's that written on the side?
8:14 AM 6th Aug 1945 from web

HiroDude Hahahahahahaha. LOL.
8:15 AM 6th Aug 1945 from web

HiroDude Hang on, what's that?
8:15 AM 6th Aug 1945 from web

HiroDude Something's fallen out the back.
8:16 AM 6th Aug 1945 from web

HiroDude What's that written on the side?
8:16 AM 6th Aug 1945 from web

HiroDude Hahahahahahaha LOL!!!
8:17 AM 6th Aug 1945 from web

HiroDude Oh shit.
8:18 AM 6th Aug 1945 from web

CaptainRobertA.Lewis On way home.
8:32 AM 6th Aug 1945 from bombdeck

CaptainRobertA.Lewis Did you see that guy laughing at us?
8:32 AM 6th Aug 1945 from bombdeck

GroupCmmndrColPaulTibbets @CaptainRobertA.Lewis Yeah.
8:33 AM 6th Aug 1945 from flitedeck

CaptainRobertA.Lewis @GroupCmmndrColPaulTibbets Told you.
8:34 AM 6th Aug 1945 from bombdeck

#FIRSTMANINSPACE

YuriAlekseyevich Hello? Anybody? I'm stuck.
8:35 AM 12th Apr 1961 from CCCPMobile

YuriAlekseyevich My name is Yuri Gagarin, I'm a cook at Baikonur Cosmodrome. I work in the kitchens. I don't know where I am. #helpyuri
8:39 AM 12th Apr 1961 from CCCPMobile

YuriAlekseyevich I'm strapped into some sort of chair and someone has put my glass mixing bowl over my head. What's going on? #helpyuri
8:41 AM 12th Apr 1961 from CCCPMobile

YuriAlekseyevich Dr. Korolev and the Air Marshal took me out for a drink last night. Last thing I remember we were knocking back the Stolichnayas #helpyuri
8:43 AM 12th Apr 1961 from CCCPMobile

YuriAlekseyevich And singing VERY rude songs #helpyuri
8.45 AM 12th Apr 1961 from CCCPMobile

YuriAlekseyevich The Air Marshal was saying something about how some missions are too dangerous to risk your best men on, and did I understand? #helpyuri
8:47 AM 12th Apr 1961 from CCCPMobile

YuriAlekseyevich I said no I didn't, and he said "good" and poured me another vodka #helpyuri
8:49 AM 12th Apr 1961 from CCCPMobile

YuriAlekseyevich After that it's all a bit foggy #helpyuri
8:50 AM 12th Apr 1961 from CCCPMobile

YuriAlekseyevich I expect this is a hearty practical joke to show I am now One Of The Guys. Yes, that'll be it. #helpyuri
8:51 AM 12th Apr 1961 from CCCPMobile

YuriAlekseyevich The Air Marshal's voice just came on the radio (at least I think it's a radio) He sounds much less hungover than me. #helpyuri
8:54 AM 12th Apr 1961 from CCCPMobile

YuriAlekseyevich The Air Marshal just called me a hero of the Soviet Union. What a relief! I thought I was in trouble. #helpyuri
8:55 AM 12th Apr 1961 from CCCPMobile

YuriAlekseyevich I hope they get me out of here soon. I've got to help make breakfast. #helpyuri
8:56 AM 12th Apr 1961 from CCCPMobile

YuriAlekseyevich The Air Marshal says the journey I'm about to take will change history. Am I being transferred? Hope it's somewhere nice #helpyuri
8:57 AM 12th Apr 1961 from CCCPMobile

YuriAlekseyevich I hear the weather's lovely in Georgia this time of year. #helpyuri
8:58 AM 12th Apr 1961 from CCCPMobile

YuriAlekseyevich Now someone's counting backwards from ten. I suppose when they get to zero they'll come and let me out. #helpyuri
8:59 AM 12th Apr 1961 from CCCPMobile

YuriAlekseyevich @AnnaGagarina
MUUUUUUUUUUMMMMMMMMMMYYYYYYYYYYY
9:01 AM 12th Apr 1961 from CCCPMobile

#THECUBAN MISSILECRISIS

jfk Anyone else wondering what Russia is up to?
2:15 PM 14th Oct 1962 from web

Khrushchev @jfk What do you mean 'what are we up to'?
12:31 PM 18th Oct 1962 from sovietwit

jfk @Krushchev I mean what the hell are you doing?
12:32 PM 18th Oct 1962 from web

Khrushchev @jfk With what?
1:56 PM 19th Oct 1962 from sovietwit

jfk @Krushchev Er.. duh.. the missiles?
2:01 PM 19th Oct 1962 from web

Khrushchev @jfk Khrushchev Oh those.
9:11 AM 20th Oct 1962 from sovietwit

jfk @Krushchev Yes those.
9:22 AM 20th Oct 1962 from web

Khrushchev @jfk Nothing.
4:13 PM 20th Oct 1962 from sovietwit

jfk @Krushchev You've put them 60 miles off our coast on Cuba!!!!1111!
4:14 PM 20th Oct 1962 from web

Khrushchev @jfk So?
2:27 PM 21st Oct 1962 from sovietwit

jfk @Krushchev What do you mean "So"?? You can't do that. And stop taking so long to answer me.
2:29 PM 21st Oct 1962 from web

Khrushchev @jfk I don't have to do what you say. You're not my dad.
9:19 PM 21st Oct 1962 from sovietwit

jfk @Krushchev Look this is completely unacceptable. We can't have a nearby Latin American country openly allying with Russia.
9:32 PM 21st Oct 1962 from web

Khrushchev @jfk Why not?
10:05 AM 22nd Oct 1962 from sovietwit

jfk @Krushchev Because of the 1945 Russo-American enmity, that's why not.
10:08 AM 22nd Oct 1962 from web

Khrushchev @jfk Well you should have thought of that before you decided to go round harassing our fellow communists.
10:10 AM 22nd Oct 1962 from sovietwit

jfk @Krushchev Bollocks. You're just trying it on.
10:12 AM 22nd Oct 1962 from web

jfk @Krushchev You know damn well it's the policy of this nation to regard any nukes launched from Cuba against any nation in the Western Hemisphere ....
10:12 AM 22nd Oct 1962 from web

jfk @Krushchev .....as an attack on the United States, requiring a full retaliatory response upon the Soviet Union.
10:12 AM 22nd Oct 1962 from web

Khrushchev @jfk Oh get stuffed.
10:31 AM 22nd Oct 1962 from sovietwit

jfk @Krushchev No YOU get stuffed.
10:33 AM 22nd Oct 1962 from web

Khrushchev @jfk No YOU get stuffed.
10:35 AM 10th Oct 1962 from sovietwit

jfk @Krushchev No YOU get stuffed.
10:35 AM 22nd Oct 1962 from web

Khrushchev @jfk No YOU get stuffed. And get f**ked as
well you twat.
10:37 AM 22nd Oct 1962 from sovietwit

jfk @Krushchev I'm f**king warning u Khruschev. One more tweet
like that and I'm blockading Cuba and your shitty little ships will be
turned back.
10:39 AM 22nd Oct 1962 from web

Khrushchev @jfk Alright, here's the deal. Unless you agree
to a non-invasion policy regarding Cuba the missiles stay.
7:35 AM 26th Oct 1962 from sovietwit

jfk @Krushchev And if I agree you'll get rid of them?
9:03 AM 26th Oct 1962 from web

Khrushchev @jfk Yes.
10:10 AM 27th Oct 1962 from sovietwit

jfk @Krushchev Fine. The place stinks anyway.
10:15 AM 27th Oct 1962 from web

Khrushchev @jfk Fine.
8:18 AM 28th Oct 1962 from sovietwit

jfk @Krushchev Fine.
8:19 AM 28th Oct 1962 from web

Khrushchev @jfk Fine.
8:47 AM 28th Oct 1962 from sovietwit

jfk @Krushchev Crisis over then.
9:00 AM 28th Oct 1962 from web

Khrushchev @jfk You're still a twat though.
9:11 AM 28th Oct 1962 from sovietwit

#THEASSASSINATION OFJOHNF.KENNEDY

jackiekennedy morning tweeters! In Dallas, TX for hubby's 'meet the people' day. Whole day driving round and round waving at everyone. BORING.
11:39 AM 22nd Nov 1963 from mrpresideck

jackiekennedy In car with Governor Connally and his wife Nellie. They seem cool. John's just suggested putting the roof down.
11:43 AM 22nd Nov 1963 from mrpresideck

jackiekennedy we're off. Probably live to regret roof down idea if it rains!
11:44 AM 22nd Nov 1963 from mrpresideck

jackiekennedy Stopped so that John can shake hands with some nuns. Loads of schoolkids screeching. And I've got the WORST headache.
12:05 PM 22nd Nov 1963 from mrpresideck

jackiekennedy Excitement! Some guy just ran towards motorcade but was dragged off by secret service! John didn't notice. Too busy with nuns.
12:10 PM 22nd Nov 1963 from mrpresideck

jackiekennedy God this is dull. I hope someone does something to liven it up a bit. Still got headache.
12:20 PM 22nd Nov 1963 from mrpresideck

jackiekennedy Just turned into some sort of plaza.
http://twitpic.com/jackiek/0876.jpg
12:29 PM 22nd Nov 1963 from mrpresideck

jackiekennedy We're all bored but able to keep smiling at the
proles coz Governor Connally just told us great joke hang on – will
RT
12:29 PM 22nd Nov 1963 from mrpresideck

jackiekennedy RT @governorconnally why should you never hit a
dwarf with learning difficulties?
12:29 PM 22nd Nov 1963 from mrpresideck

jackiekennedy wait for punchline – honestly this will kill you!
12:29 PM 22nd Nov 1963 from mrpresideck

jackiekennedy Hang on – what the F**K was THAT? Was that a
car backfiring?
12:31 PM 22nd Nov 1963 from mrpresideck

jackiekennedy Shit shit shit shit shit shit shit
12:31 PM 22nd Nov 1963 from mrpresideck

jackiekennedy shit shit shit shit shit shit
12:31 PM 22nd Nov 1963 from mrpresideck

jackiekennedy RT @governorconnally shit shit shit shit shit shit
12:31 PM 22nd Nov 1963 from mrpresideck

jackiekennedy oh man, just been shot at and john's been
hit!!!!111! In the neck I think but he's still alive.
12:32 *PM 22nd Nov 1963 from* mrpresideck

jackiekennedy Oh. Scratch that.
12:32 PM 22nd Nov 1963 from mrpresideck

jackiekennedy RT @governorconnally nearest hospital is
Parkland Memorial – hurry!
12:32 PM 22nd Nov 1963 from mrpresideck

jackiekennedy Man this is going to cost a fortune in dry cleaning.
12:32 PM 22nd Nov 1963 from mrpresideck

jackiekennedy Climbing across back of limo onto trunk. Is that
a bit of SKULL??? Man this is f**ked up!
12:32 PM 22nd Nov 1963 from mrpresideck

jackiekennedy kind of puts my headache of earlier into
perspective.
12:33 PM 22nd Nov 1963 from mrpresideck

jackiekennedy Can't tweet. Need both hands to hold bits.
Gotta go.
12:33 PM 22nd Nov 1963 from mrpresideck

jackiekennedy Almost forgot! RT @govenorconnally It's not big and
it's not clever LOL!!
12:34 PM 22nd Nov 1963 from mrpresideck

#JOHNLENNON

JohnLennon I never said we were bigger than Jesus, I said we were bigger than Jesús, the little guy who used to clean the pool when we were in Florida.
1:12 PM 11th Aug 11 1966 from BeatleBerry

JohnLennon What I said was "we've got a bigger VAN than Jesus". We've got a big bus now and the Salvation Army still drive round in little Bedfords.
1:14 PM 11th Aug 1966 from BeatleBerry

JohnLennon I was GONNA say we were bigger than Freddie & The Dreamers, then a car backfires, I shout JESUS and Maureen Cleave writes it down, daft cow.
1:16 PM 11th Aug 1966 from BeatleBerry

JohnLennon When I said we were bigger than Jesus, I just meant we've got a combined height of nearly 23 feet. Jesus can't have been bigger than that.
1:18 PM 11th Aug 1966 from BeatleBerry

#MOONLANDING

BUZZMAN I had first dibs on the seat by the door, I KNOW I did.
6:12 PM 19th Jul 1969 from BuzzBerry

Armstrongn1 I hope Buzz doesn't remember he called first dibs on this seat.
6:13 PM 19th Jul 1969 from MoonWeb

BUZZMAN I was just about to sit down when Neil's all like "Hey buddy is that your left wrist seal open?"
6:13 PM 19th Jul 1969 from BuzzBerry

Armstrongn1 I can't believe he fell for that open wrist seal thing, lol (quietly).
6:14 PM 19th Jul 1969 from MoonWeb

BUZZMAN So I check the seal, it's fine OF COURSE and when I look backj the little bitch is in my seat.
6:14 PM 19th Jul 1969 from BuzzBerry

Armstrongn1 He's not saying anything but he's not happy. His eyes look like cat's assholes.
6:15 PM 19th Jul 1969 from MoonWeb

BUZZMAN We've been arguing about this for weeks, I thought we'd figured it out but NOOO.
6:16 PM 19th Jul 1969 from BuzzBerry

Armstrongn1 Hey, I came up with the "One small step" spiel, I should be the one gets to say it, right?
6:18 PM 19th Jul 1969 from MoonWeb

BUZZMAN Just 'cos he thinks he came up with the One Small Step thing. Made no sense at all till I rewrote it for him.
6:20 PM 19th Jul 1969 from BuzzBerry

Armstrongn1 Can you imagine how it would have sounded in that dumb high-pitched voice of his? Onesmallstepforamaneeweeweeweeweewee.
6:21 PM 19th Jul 1969 from MoonWeb

BUZZMAN One Big Jump for people. That was what he wanted to say. BIG JUMP FOR PEOPLE. Jesus.
6:21 PM 19th Jul 1969 from BuzzBerry

Armstrongn1 Fun though this is, someone has to go be first man on the moon, namely the guy in the seat by the door, as in – well whaddya know...
6:23 PM 19th Jul 1969 from MoonWeb

BUZZMAN Go on, dickwad, see if I care. Hope you fall off the damn ladder and crack your faceplate.
6:23 PM 19th Jul 1969 from BuzzBerry

BUZZMAN OMG HE BLEW IT! It's A man! Small step for A man! One line and he f**ked it! LO-OOSER! HA!
6:24 PM 19th Jul 1969 from BuzzBerry

theothermichaelcollins Boy I hope those two take their time down there. Sure is peaceful in the orbiter without them.
6:30 PM 19th Jul 1969 from SpaceNet

#FALLOFTHE BERLINWALL

KlausF There's a rumour going round that the East German govt. is opening the border – more news as & when #berlin
9:14 AM 9th Nov 1989 from WestWeb

KlausF It looks like it's true – the checkpoint guards are just waving everyone through – is this it? Is it over? #berlin
5:12 PM 9th Nov 1989 from WestWeb

KlausF The most joyous day – the Ossis are flooding into West Berlin – people are dancing on the wall – you have to see this #berlin
10:04 AM 10th Nov 1989 from WestWeb

KlausF People attacking the wall with any tools they can find – a huge crack has opened and Ossis are pouring through & hugging Wessis #berlin
1:25 PM 11th Nov 1989 from WestWeb

KlausF David Hasselhoff is here! He's singing on the wall! #berlin
10:25 PM 31st Dec 1989 from WestWeb

KlausF The Ossis are pouring BACK through the hole in the wall and trying to fix it with chewing gum #berlin
10:29 PM 31st Dec 1989 from WestWeb

#THEDEATHOF PRINCESSDIANA

princephillip @headofmi5 No No No you blithering idiot I tweeted "we could just kill her and make it look like an accident – NOT".
4:05 AM 31st Aug 1997 from conspiritweet

princephillip @headofmi5 The NOT got left off.
4:05 AM 31st Aug 1997 from conspiritweet

princephillip @headofmi5 Bloody 140 character limit.
4:05 AM 31st Aug 1997 from conspiritweet

#THESPECIAL RELATIONSHIP

TonyBlairPM @GeorgeW Hi, Mr. President, sorry to disturb but I've tried the hotline and there's been no reply.
4:12 PM 19th Feb 2003 from NumberTenNet

GeorgeW @TonyBlairPM hay ther tony sory I never got yr call but they moved the fone to a nother office on acount i kept usin it fer prank calls.
4:14 PM 19th Feb 2003 from WWeb

TonyBlairPM @GeorgeW The thing is we really need to go over initial troop provisions for Operation Iraqi Freedom as my lot are sure there aren't enough.
4:15 PM 19th Feb 2003 from NumberTenNet

GeorgeW @TonyBlairPM You know, you fone a bar or sumfin and say Im Lookin fer Mr Ock 1st name Mike so the guy shouts out Anybody Seen Mike Ock pmsl!
4:17 PM 19th Feb 2003 from WWeb

TonyBlairPM @GeorgeW Sounds lovely.
4:22 PM 19th Feb 2003 from NumberTenNet

GeorgeW @TonyBlairPM Hey listen nex time yr over we'll try prank callin the UN. Tell em were about to bom China LOL.
4:21 PM 19th Feb 2003 from WWeb

TonyBlairPM @GeorgeW Is there anyone else there I can talk to?
4:18 PM 19th Feb 2003 from NumberTenNet